101 PLAYGROUND GAMES

101 Playground Games is a collection of active and engaging school playground games for children. It offers enriching activities and traditional games to encourage active learning and social development among young children at playtime.

The school playground plays a crucial role in developing all aspects of children's behaviour and interpersonal learning, and yet there is a growing awareness that children today do not play in the same sociable ways as previous generations. This fully updated second edition draws on traditional games and introduces a wealth of new ones, including:

- traditional games
- tag games
- chasing and catching games
- singing and dancing games
- skipping games and rhymes
- circle games
- parachute games
- quiet games
- co-operative games
- games from around the world

This resource provides a practical toolkit of ideas to promote lively and enjoyable games and provides clear instructions for adults on how to organise the games. It is a book that will make any playtime a richer experience for all.

Thérèse Hoyle has over 25 years' experience teaching in mainstream, special and higher education and has worked as an education consultant, coach, wellbeing adviser and trainer with over 495 schools and organisations. She is recognised as the UK's leading training provider of playtime and lunchtime programmes with her 'How to Be a Lunchtime Supervisor Superhero' workshop and 'Positive Playtime' Masterclasses.

101 PLAYGROUND GAMES

SECOND EDITION

A COLLECTION OF
ACTIVE AND ENGAGING
PLAYTIME GAMES
FOR CHILDREN

Thérèse Hoyle

Routledge
Taylor & Francis Group

LONDON AND NEW YORK

Second edition published 2021
by Routledge
2 Park Square, Milton Park, Abingdon, Oxon, OX14 4RN

and by Routledge
605 Third Avenue, New York, NY 10158

Routledge is an imprint of the Taylor & Francis Group, an informa business

© 2021 Thérèse Hoyle

First edition published by Optimus Education 2008

British Library Cataloguing-in-Publication Data
A catalogue record for this book is available from the British Library

Library of Congress Cataloging-in-Publication Data
Names: Hoyle, Thérèse, author.
Title: 101 playground games: a collection of active and engaging playtime games for children/Thérèse Hoyle.
Other titles: One hundred and one playground games
Description: Second edition. | Abingdon, Oxon; New York, NY: Routledge, 2021. | Includes bibliographical references and index.
Identifiers: LCCN 2020055442 (print) | LCCN 2020055443 (ebook) | ISBN 9781032012063 (hardback) | ISBN 9780367338565 (paperback) | ISBN 9780429322396 (ebook)
Subjects: LCSH: Outdoor games. | Outdoor recreation. | Playgrounds. | Social skills in children.
Classification: LCC GV1203 .H74 2021 (print) | LCC GV1203 (ebook) | DDC 796–dc23
LC record available at https://lccn.loc.gov/2020055442
LC ebook record available at https://lccn.loc.gov/2020055443

ISBN: 978-1-032-01206-3 (hbk)
ISBN: 978-0-367-33856-5 (pbk)
ISBN: 978-0-429-32239-6 (ebk)

Typeset in Futura
by Deanta Global Publishing Services, Chennai, India

Access the Support Material: www.routledge.com/9780367338565

This book is dedicated to Amber, my playful daughter. Thank you for being you, for your amazingly playful nature and for inspiring and laughing with me over the years as we played many of the games contained within this book. I am so grateful for you cheerleading and supporting me with my work in education, it means so much. I am truly blessed to call you my daughter and appreciate all the joy you bring into this world.

Contents

Using the Online Resource

Many Speechmark publications include online resources to support the purchaser in the delivery of the training or teaching activities. These may include any of the following file formats:

- PDFs requiring Acrobat v.3

- Microsoft Word files

- The appendices are included in the online resource available from www.routledge.com/9780367338565

This material is available online and can be printed by the purchaser/user of the book. This includes library copies. The online version must not be reproduced or copied in its entirety for use by others without permission from the publisher.

All material in the online resource is © Hoyle 2020.

Symbol Key

 These symbols indicate pages that can be photocopied from the book or printed from the online resource.

 Traditional Playground Games

 Tag Games

 Chasing and Catching Games

 Singing and Dancing Games

 Skipping Games and Rhymes

 Circle Games

 Parachute Games

 Quiet Games

 Co-Operative Games

 Games from Around the World

Acknowledgements

A huge thank you to everyone who bought a copy of my first edition *101 Playground Games*. I regularly meet teachers and school leaders who tell me they have the book and it never ceases to surprise and delight me. Thank you for buying my book. I think you will agree we have an even better second edition!

Since 1998 I have worked nationally and internationally with over 495 schools and organisations and with more than 15,400 individuals and countless numbers of children! I have learnt so much on my journey and am so grateful to all the children, teachers, headteachers, lunchtime supervisors, teaching assistants and parents, breakfast and after school club leaders; cub, scout, brownie and guide leaders; thank you for making this book a possibility.

I would particularly like to thank Jane Cook, former headteacher of Honeywell Infants, and Firs Farm Primary School in London, where I started my first playground projects and to the many other British schools and local education authorities I have worked with since. I would also like to thank all the New Zealand schools I worked with between 2002 and 2009 for embracing my ideas and running effortlessly with my Positive Playtime and Flourishing Schools programmes and the many other international schools I've had the pleasure to travel to, consult and train with.

I am particularly grateful to the children at St Joseph's School, Queenstown, New Zealand, Colmers Farm Primary School, Birmingham, and Great Malvern Primary School, Malvern, for letting me test games out on you and for teaching me new ones. I learnt so much in the process and it was great fun! Thank you to Amber, my daughter for letting your (sometimes crazy) mother test games out on you and your friends. I know you weren't always sure about having me in your school playground. I also appreciate your friends teaching me Four Square, which I have added to this book!

Julia McCutchen was my writing coach, back in 2008, when my first edition was published. She gave me the courage to write my first book and get over my imposter syndrome! Thank you for sharing your wisdom and keeping me on track!

Thank you to my encouraging and supportive editors George Robinson and the late Barbara Maines, for my first edition 101 Playground Games. You made my dream a reality. Your gentle, thoughtful and considered responses to my writing and your encouragement and suggestions were very much appreciated. It was a real pleasure working with you.

Acknowledgements

Thank you to Katrina Hulme Cross and her team at Routledge for agreeing to publish a second edition of *101 Playground Games* and to my current editors Sarah Hyde and Will Bateman who have supported me tirelessly with my vision and all my questions and queries. It has been a pure delight working with you and I so appreciate that you have listened to all my ideas and supported me with making the book look exactly how I had envisioned! It has been a joyful collaboration with you both and I appreciate that you involved me in every step of the process, from writing to publication. Thank you.

Thank you to Neil Hawkes for your commitment to Values-based Education (VbE), your friendship over 25 years and your amazing foreword; it made me cry! To Sam Yeomans, whom I met when I worked at Colmers Farm Primary School and who ran an after school club teaching playground games from my book! You have really supported this second edition and I'm so grateful to you. Thank you to Karen Boyes from Spectrum Education New Zealand; you wholeheartedly supported my work in New Zealand and continue to do so to this day with my contributions to your *Teacher Matter Magazine*, a recent feature on Spectrum TV talking about how to create a positive playtime and support of my second edition book.

With huge gratitude to my Mum for always believing in me, my daughter for her enthusiasm and encouragement of my work in education, my partner Rob for celebrating every milestone towards this second edition and supporting my vision and Snowy our dog who has sat patiently in his basket, at my feet, while I've been researching and writing. With all your love and support, my dream of leaving a legacy, where these games can be passed onto the next generation, has become a reality – thank you.

Foreword

I recommend that each school should have a Thérèse Hoyle on its staff to ensure that children have access to the joy and learning contained in this outstanding book.

Reading her superb and comprehensive book about playground games has awakened my imagination, which has run wild as I have remembered the pleasures of the playground games experienced during my own childhood. I became an eight-year-old again playing What's the Time Mr Wolf? at Lethbridge Road Primary School in Swindon. Characters from my childhood were remembered, as I saw myself playing Stuck in the Mud. Thank you, Thérèse!

During my long career as an educator, I have had the privilege of visiting what now must amount to thousands of schools in many parts of the world. I have learned much from my visits, but most of all I have learned of the importance of play as the foundation of the curriculum in primary schools. What I consider to be the best schools, give a range of first-hand experiences to children, which include four golden keys: being immersed in experiencing and understanding nature, leaning about values, realising the importance of developing and maintaining relationships and experiencing the joy of play. These four keys result in a human being who is truly educated: observant, curious, knowledgeable, altruistic, compassionate, joyful and playful.

I am blessed with grandchildren. Recently five of them, ranging in age from 4 to 11, were walking with me on the Chiltern Hill, when suddenly a game began, which was a form of Mr Wolf, using crunchy fallen beech leaves for Mr Wolf to scatter over us. For ten minutes we laughed until tears poured down our faces, as we experienced the spontaneity of play and the total absorption of each other's company. We appreciated too the colour and beauty of the fallen leaves – nature's joyful gift to us.

Not all children live in families and communities that encourage games, perhaps because living conditions are not conducive for outdoor group games. It is therefore so very important that schools provide adequate time and resources for playground games. In some schools, playtime has been reduced to concentrate more on the so-called formal curriculum. This, in my opinion, is a huge educational mistake and an assault on children and their natural development.

Foreword

With the demands of social distancing during social and health crises, such as the COVID-19 pandemic, schools have to be even more imaginative to enable children to experience the richness of playground games. Thérèse's unique book is a must-have book for schools and a wonderful resource for families and community groups working with children.

Dr Neil Hawkes
Founder of VbE
www.valuesbasededucation.com

Thérèse Hoyle is the UK's leading training provider of playtime and lunchtime programmes to primary schools. She is well known for her Whole School Positive Playtime and How to Be a Lunchtime Supervisor Superhero training programmes that are available as INSET, Working In School Days and as online training. She is the bestselling author of *101 Playground Games* and *101 Wet Playtime Games and Activities* and contributing author to *How to Be a Peaceful School*.

Thérèse is a sought-after speaker at workshops and conferences nationally and internationally and her work is regularly featured in the media and education journals.

For further information contact:

therese@theresehoyle.com

www.theresehoyle.com

Introduction

Children treasure their playtimes and lunchtime breaks; in fact for most children it is the best time in their day. Through play, they develop and build relationships, learn social skills, de-stress and let off steam, exercise and most of all they have fun. There are some for whom playtime can be the most challenging time in the day, a time when they may be left out of games, have nobody to play with and get bullied or called names.

In some schools, instead of the playground being a place of positive social and physical activity, it has become an unstructured, hostile environment with a lack of co-operative play and children frequently involved in aggressive play and anti-social behaviour.

This book is intended to provide you and the children with a toolkit of ideas that will enhance and enrich any playtime.

My mission is to help you re-invigorate your playtimes and to support schools with making playtimes and lunchtimes a harmonious and joyful time in the school day.

For over 20 years I have been developing, refining and running my Whole School Positive Playtime and How to Be a Lunchtime Supervisor Superhero programmes, as well as writing my best selling first edition of *101 Playground Games* and *101 Wet Playtime Games* and becoming a contributing author to *How to Be a Peaceful School* (2018) with a chapter called 'Peaceful Playtimes'.

My involvement in turning concrete jungles into happy play spaces started in the South London school called Honeywell. As a teacher, I regularly spent large chunks of precious learning time resolving playground squabbles that spilled over into the classroom. Upset children returned to lessons in an emotional state. Many of them were unable to learn for the rest of the afternoon. I saw the negative impact of unstructured playtimes and lack of co-operative play and realised that chaotic lunchtimes were harming the wellbeing and self-esteem of our children and that something had to change.

I was lucky enough to have a supportive headteacher, Jane Cook, who agreed to my plans and Honeywell's playground transformation took place! I then developed a passion for supporting other schools and in 1998, ran my first ten-day playground project in an inner-city London school called Firs Farm Primary. To this day, I have visions of myself as a heavily pregnant first-time mum, sitting cross-legged on the concrete playground playing Duck, Duck, Goose!

Introduction

Over my time of working with schools, I have discovered that children just want to have fun and are eager to play and learn new games. Once I start a game, I almost always have the whole school joining in.

Games have the capacity to be hugely inclusive of all children, no matter what age, culture, race, creed or ability. They offer opportunities for everyone in the school playground to get involved. Le Fevre (2007) comments that 'Games create a universal language with which people can relate to each other'.

The evaluations, from training I run in schools, frequently reveal that through playing playground games, children are happier, have fewer grievances when they return to the classroom, are more playful and co-operative and playtimes are a harmonious time in the day for everyone.

We know from research that when children have a happy playtime, they learn better in the afternoon. An added bonus I continue to hear from schools is how much happier their lunchtime supervisors, teaching assistants and teachers are, walking calmly into the staff room after play commenting on their happy playtime, so it's not just the children who benefit – we all do!

I had a lovely email from a headteacher I worked with:

> A neighbour of the school approached me over the holidays to say that she enjoys hearing the kids out in the playground when she is in the garden. And she is out there a lot! But she says in the last 18 months there has been a recognisable change in the sound of the children in the playground. She couldn't pinpoint it but said the kids sounded happier!
>
> *Brent Caldwell, headteacher*

If the benefit of more active playtimes is increased happiness, then it's well worth the investment!

Some years ago, when my daughter was young, I booked an appointment for her to attend at playtime, thinking at least she wouldn't miss any learning time! When I explained I needed to pick her up at playtime, she was distraught: 'How could you take me out of school at such a fun time in the day!' She reminded me about the importance of play and how much children value their playtime and free time. Interestingly, when children and young people are asked about what they think is important in their lives, playing and friends are consistently at the top of the list and Amber was no exception to this.

Children in the UK attend primary school for seven to eight years, and these are also their peak playing years, the running, skipping, jumping, hopping, clapping and 'mucking around' years when they become immersed in their own culture and play. It is a once-in-a-lifetime experience and as educators we can take heart knowing that games are not only good fun, but they are also of great educational value.

Play England (2021) describes play as 'an essential part of every child's life and is vital for the enjoyment of childhood as well as social, emotional, intellectual and physical development'.

Why Encourage Children to Play Games?

It is becoming increasingly evident that play and playing games is beneficial to child wellbeing.

As Harry Burns, former Chief Medical Officer of Scotland, states, 'Investing in children's play is one of the most important things we can do to improve children's health and wellbeing'.

Furthermore, a recent clinical report, *The Power of Play*, from The American Academy of Pediatrics (AAP) (Garner et al., 2018) comments on the importance of play and states, 'the importance of playful learning for children cannot be overemphasized'. According to the AAP, play is not frivolous, rather play is 'vital for brain building', a central part of healthy child development, a key to executive function skills, 'play allows for increased cognitive functioning/improving academic skills, relationships (social-emotional resilience) and helps children, "buffer toxic stress"'.

Why Encourage Children to Play Games?

The report recommends that doctors write a prescription for play because 'play is fundamentally important for developing a suite of 21st century skills, including social, emotional, language and cognitive skills, all needed by the next generation in an economically competitive world that requires collaboration and innovation'.

This report also states, 'the most powerful way children learn isn't only in classrooms or libraries but rather on playgrounds and in playrooms'. It goes on to say that 'Educators, pediatricians and families should advocate for and protect play and playful learning in preschools and schools because of its numerous benefits'.

Dr Stuart Brown (2010) founder of the National Institute of Play states in his book, *Play*, that 'play is anything but trivial. It is a biological drive as integral to our health as sleep or nutrition. In fact, our ability to play throughout life is the single most important factor in determining our success and happiness'.

In the fields of psychology and education, research has provided substantial evidence to support the role of play in communication, language and literacy learning, emotional and social development, including social competence and peer group affiliation, spatial and mathematical learning, creativity, the development of positive learning dispositions and orientations and the formation of identity (Broadhead, 2004; Frost et al., 2005; Johnson et al., 2005; Wood and Atfield, 2005). Emerging evidence on the neuro-physiological development of the brain also indicates the importance of children making connections between areas of learning and experience through play, exploration and experimentation and through collaborative, reciprocal relationships (Gopnik et al., 1999).

Lester and Russell (2008) completed a review for Play England called *Play for a Change* which further illustrates substantial and wide-ranging evidence of the importance of play in the lives of children. The review quotes Burghardt (2005) and Sutton-Smith (2003) who expand on the links with neuroscience and identify how play provides a safe way to learn about emotions:

> Much of the evidence from neuroscience suggests that, rather than developing specific skills that may be needed later in adult life, playing is a way of building and shaping regions of the brain that concern emotion, motivation and reward, and developing a range of flexible responses across a number of adaptive systems that link the brain, the body and the social and physical environment.
>
> *(Burghardt, 2005)*

> First hand experience of the raw emotions of joy, fear, anger, sadness, shock and disgust are essential for these processes to take place, and are evident in these kinds of playing. Play provides a relatively safe context in which these primary emotions can be expressed, while being held in check by the rules, rituals and play signals of the game.

These rules, rituals and play signals are, in turn driven by the more social, secondary emotions such as pride, shame and sympathy.

(Sutton-Smith, 2003)

Lester and Russell (2008) also highlight the importance of play as a way of building resilience:

> Play can help build resilience – the capacity for children to thrive despite adversity and stress in their lives. Emotions have a key role in playing and play makes a major contribution to developing emotion regulation, building strong attachments and peer friendships, engendering positive feelings, and enabling children to cope with stressful situations through developing creative approaches and problem-solving.

According to the Mental Health Foundation (2021), having time and the freedom to play indoors and outdoors can help keep children and young people mentally well.

Sunderland (2016), a British child psychotherapist, director of education and training at the Centre for Child Mental Health and director of Trauma Informed Schools, points clearly to the fact that, for many reasons, physical interactive play is important to long-term mental and emotional health. This form of play has natural anti-stress effects and because it strongly releases opioids, it promotes powerful emotional states. Interactive play can enhance the emotion-regulating functions of the frontal lobes, helping children to manage their feelings better.

What Happens If Children Don't Get Enough Play?

Panksepp (1993), a neuroscientist and psychologist, says 'We ignore play at our peril. Research shows that if infants don't get enough socially interactive play, they will make up for lost time and play harder often at the wrong times'. In other words, their play impulse comes out inappropriately. This is what can happen with some children labelled as having attention deficit hyperactivity disorder (ADHD). One study found that children deprived of playtime at school developed ADHD symptoms and were unable to sit still and focus their attention (Pellegrini et al., 1996). Panksepp and Ikemoto (1992), explain this further:

> In ADHD, one major problem is that the frontal lobes are not yet fully 'online'. Interactive play can develop a child's frontal lobes and enhance their regulating functions. This helps an ADHD child to naturally inhibit her primitive 'motoric impulses' (all that rushing about, wanting to hit you) and manage stressful situations.

Why Encourage Children to Play Games?

If children don't get enough play they also end up with what Stuart Brown (2010) describes as a 'serious play deficit, much like the well documented sleep deficit', which subsequently impacts social, emotional, mental and physical health and wellbeing.

The Benefits of Playtime Games for Child Health and Wellbeing

We know from research that when children and young adults run around in the playground and play games, it improves their physical health and wellbeing.

Playtime offers children an important opportunity to increase their physical wellbeing through 'unstructured physical activity' (World Health Organisation, 2021).

As Charles Basch (2011) comments in his report, *Healthier Students Make Better Learners*,

> Physical activity has dramatic effects on individuals physical and mental health.

Sadly, our child obesity levels are rising, and current statistics show that 20 per cent of Year 6 children are classified as obese (NHS England, 2020). The World Health Organisation regards childhood obesity as one of the most serious global public health challenges of the 21st century.

In the book *How to Be a Peaceful School*, Hoyle (2018) comments:

> Obese children are more likely to develop childhood diabetes along with various other health problems. This along with the news that doctors have started prescribing vitamin D tablets to children following an upsurge in the number of children developing rickets (through lack of sunshine) is astonishing, when playing outside offers a simple and easy way to significantly reduce the chances of experiencing these health problems.

The finding to child health and wellbeing of Davey (2006) regarding traditional games may be of significance:

> Traditional games have been found to be of major importance for children's physical and mental development and wellbeing. Two physical education lecturers, Peter L. Lindsay and Denise Palmer (1981), carried out a study in Brisbane. It showed that in many respects traditional games were more beneficial to children's health (for example, their cardio-vascular endurance) than formal syllabus games.

Paediatric research (Health Education Authority, 1997; Armstrong and Welsman, 1997; Bouchard et al., 1997) recognises that numerous health and fitness gains are associated with physical play and general physical activity. Physical play and activity:

- help to regulate body weight

- lead to increased bone density and mineralisation

- lead to improved ability to use fat for energy

- help to regulate blood pressure

Others have pointed to the contribution that physical play and physical activity make to the wider aspects of 'quality of life' such as those associated with mental and emotional health. Dishman (1986), for example, found regular physical activity is associated with a reduction in anxiety, stress and mild to moderate depression across all ages and both genders.

Further findings suggest that a physically active lifestyle is associated with improved self-esteem and self-concept (Gruber, 1986).

Research however shows the free time available within school during breaktimes is clearly being underutilised in the context of promoting physical activity (Waring et al., 2007).

There are many studies (Burdette and Whittaker, 2005; Verstraete, 2006) that call for schools to encourage more physical activity and game playing during school lunchtimes and playtimes.

A longer playtime would allow children to gain the most benefit from physical activity, as studies have suggested that higher physical activity levels are associated with longer playtimes (Ridgers et al., 2007; Parish, 2013).

It is therefore imperative schools encourage playing games as a form of exercise; and the activities in this book, such as tag games and skipping, promote cardiovascular health and suit all ability levels.

What is noticeable when I am outside playing games with children is the freedom that children experience to really be themselves and the incredible joy that games bring. There is evidence that by making children feel brighter and happier, games can prevent illness. Studies now show that prolonged dark feelings actually harm the body and cause disease.

Psychologist Dr Robert Holden (1999) states,

> The child who does not play, runs the risk of serious setback in life. This setback will manifest itself, physically, emotionally, mentally, and spiritually... Play can be a natural therapy, a medicine and a natural healer that promotes humour, happiness and wholeness. An absence of fun, little or no playtime and a lack of laughter are common symptoms of stress, sickness, and disease. Little or no time for play can also be a significant cause of illness and disharmony. On the other hand, frequent prescriptions of play can inspire rest, relaxation and recovery. Play is also an act of 're-creation'. Through play we can recharge, revitalise and re-energise ourselves back into life.

Why Encourage Children to Play Games?

Sunderland (2016) further substantiates these findings,

> The activation of the brain's play system is key to living well. When this system is optimally activated in childhood, it is likely to set vital foundations for the ability in later life to bring fun and a sense of play into relationships. The 'play urge' can be channeled into vital social capacities. Also in adulthood when the play system works in combination with the higher verbal brain, it is likely to result in new forms of play, such as humour and the play of ideas, a kind of 'playground of the mind'. Humour is a vital capacity for mental health in the face of adversity.

The playground is where children learn basic relationship skills such as taking turns and how to get along with others; they learn to negotiate rules, co-operate and make sure that disputes don't get out of hand, all without the intervention of us adults.

There are many benefits of playing games to the health and wellbeing of children. In fact, it would appear preposterous and inconceivable to not include play in their lives.

Below is a list which consolidates some of the above points and includes some additional benefits.

The benefits of play:

- increased physical health and wellbeing

- increased social, emotional and mental health and wellbeing

- strengthening and development of friendships

- improved cognitive development

- increased resilience

- improved emotional responsiveness

- teamwork and camaraderie

- fun and joy

- the promotion of children's development, learning, imagination, creativity and independence

- the opportunity for children to experience and encounter boundaries

- stress reduction

- language development

- the development of confidence and self-esteem

We want our children to be running, engaging, giggling and smiling for their one-and-a-quarter hour of playtime every school day. Their health and wellbeing will be significantly stronger as a result.

How Much Time Do Children Spend Playing?

It is important to consider the amount of time children spend playing in the playground.

In the United Kingdom, primary school children can spend up to 20% of their school day, or 1.4 years of their school attendance, in the playground. Over the course of their primary schooling, from Reception to Year 6, children spend over 1,600 hours playing, which equates to 260 school days. That is significant, and it may make you re-think the investment you put into your playgrounds, playtimes and time spent playing games.

Over a school year

244 hours

39 days

7.8 weeks

Primary Years

1.4 years

School day **Play time**

Note: Assumes a school day is 9 a.m. to 3.15 p.m. and there are 195 days in a school year.

Playtime Challenges

Play has been consistently undervalued in public policy for children, which tends to focus on children's development into adulthood while overlooking the importance of the physical, social, cultural and emotional worlds that children both inhabit and create in their daily lives.

(Lester and Russell, 2008)

Many headteachers, teachers, teaching assistants and lunchtime supervisors share with me the challenges of creating a happy, positive playtime with children struggling with friendship issues, bullying and boredom because of a lack of resources and some children just not knowing how to play. The truth is that many schools struggle with this time in the school day.

Over the years of running Positive Playtime projects globally, I have spoken with thousands of children in circle times about their school experiences, and they have often shared their positive experiences as well as their worries, fears and concerns about what happens at playtimes.

Their worries fall into the following categories:

- Friendship – lack of friends, being left out of games, asking to play a game and being told 'no, they can't join in', friends being unkind and arguing.

- Lack of things to do – boredom stemming from lack of resources, games, equipment and things to do in the playground.

- Feeling unsafe – physical and verbal aggression.

Research shows us 75 per cent of bullying in schools happens in the school playground (Smith and Sharp, 1994) and one of the suggested causes is boredom or lack of stimulus. Research also tells us that children are four times more likely to be bullied in the school playground than online and that sadly 50 per cent of students who are bullied don't tell their teachers and when asked why, students say they are scared teachers may make the situation worse. The effects of bullying can have painful and lifelong consequences.

As educators, we all want our children to be safe, and we aren't always aware when there is an emotional barrier to learning, which can happen if a child has a bad playtime and lunchtime. Those feelings and experiences can be taken back into the classroom after lunch and it can be hard for the child to engage in schoolwork with all their thoughts still focused on the challenges they've experienced.

With Ofsted requirements around safeguarding, pupil behaviour, discipline, relationships, child welfare, quality teaching and learning, creating a safe, peaceful, nurturing school is vital to our children achieving their potential.

Children Don't Know How to Play

During the years that I have run Positive Playtime training courses, a frequent cry from teachers and lunchtime supervisors has been that children just don't know how to play and that they no longer play the old traditional games that we used to play. They say, 'It wasn't like this in our day, children knew how to play. We played street games, the roads were safe, and we didn't have screens!'

The media, educators and government report that many of our children have lost the art of knowing how to play.

A Play England study (Lester and Russell 2007 & 2008) of children between the ages of 7 and 16 found that classic childhood games barely featured, with only six per cent of children naming playing Hide and Seek as their favourite pastime. Instead, their favourite pastime was socialising. If children have lost the art of knowing how to play, then I would suggest that perhaps these are some further reasons.

Why Children Have Lost the Art of Knowing How to Play?

• Lack of playing fields and children's recreation areas

Since 1991, over 5,000 playing fields have been sold and local authorities across the country have also been closing down children's playgrounds.

• Parental anxiety and fears for children's safety

Parental anxiety is preventing many children from playing outside unsupervised – even though most adults enjoyed this freedom themselves as children. Play Day (2007) carried out comprehensive research and found that while 71 per cent of adults played in the street or area near their home every day when they were a child, only 21 per cent of children do so today.

Their research shows that many parents prevent children from experiencing the rough and tumble of outdoor play and worry that their neighbours will look down on them if they allow their children to play outdoors unsupervised. Fifty-three per cent of parents fear the danger posed by traffic, while others are afraid their child will be snatched by a stranger. Tim Gill (2007) in his book, *No Fear*, comments that the fear of 'stranger danger' is disproportionate to the risk, as crime figures are relatively unchanged over the decades. 'The fear therefore has more to do with irresponsible and sensationalist media coverage'.

• Lack of outdoor space and no gardens

Interestingly, during the coronavirus (COVID-19) lockdown, when there was a serious concern for children to be playing and getting outside, the Ordnance Survey (OS) map data (May 2020) revealed that one in eight households (12 per cent) in Great Britain has no access to a private or shared garden.

• Lack of time

Children seem to have less and less time to play, with screen time for five-to-ten-year-olds now taking up about four-and-a-half hours a day, and homework one hour (Follett, 2017).

Why Encourage Children to Play Games?

A survey of 2,000 parents in the United Kingdom (The Guardian, 2016) found that nearly three-quarters of children are spending less than one hour outside every day. That is less time outside than prison inmates, who get two hours. About 20 per cent are not going outside, at all, on a regular basis. Yet, two in five youngsters say they are desperate to spend more time outside.

Changes in Society

Further reasons why children have lost the art of knowing how to play may be linked to changes in society, which include:

- the development of technology, which has seen children watching television and playing on screens instead of going outside.

- many much smaller families, which means children have fewer brothers and sisters to play with.

- many parents working long hours and having less time and energy to play with their children.

- the pressure on non-curricular activities with the demands of testing and results.

- schools shortening playtimes and some abolishing playtime altogether.

I have worked in schools internationally and lived overseas. This has given me an understanding of education globally and has provided me with an insight into the many schools that are challenged to the hilt with aggressive and anti-social playground behaviour and the pressure on them to increase teaching time and 'fit' the curriculum in. In a bid to try and manage behaviour and meet government targets around children's learning, an emerging and worrying trend has appeared where schools are encouraged to shorten or disband play altogether.

Shortening Playtimes – Whatever Happened to Recess?

In most schools I work in, playtimes has been shortened from the 65 minutes children used to have in the 1990s to 30 minutes with the rest of the time being taken up with eating lunch and lining up. Afternoon's play also seems to have sadly disappeared.

Baines and Blatchford (Nuffield Foundation, 2019) found that 'there has been a reduction in the length of breaktimes since 2006 and a really marked decline since 1995'.

The main reasons they found for the reduction in break times 'are to create more time for teaching and learning, specifically to cover the curriculum and to manage or limit perceived poor behaviour of students that school staff say occurs during lunchtimes'.

There are some schools, who in their striving for excellence and academic success, have subjugated play for more academic and intellectual pursuits.

Dr Michael Patte presented a paper to The Association for the Study of Play Conference in Canada. His paper was entitled 'What's Happened to Recess?' ('recess' is a term used to describe playtime in the USA). He looked at free playtime in Pennsylvania's elementary schools. Patte discussed the alarming decimation of children's play in many schools in the United States. He quoted from the American Association for the Child's Right to Play, which states that:

> Since 1990, 40% of the nation's 16,000 school districts have either modified, deleted or are considering deleting recess from the daily elementary school schedule due to increased pressure from numerous sources to improve academic achievement.

Ron Schachter reported in his article 'The End of Recess' that up to 40 per cent of school districts in California had reduced or eliminated recess to make more time for academic learning.

We should not forget Article 31 of the United Nations Convention on the Rights of the Child (1989),

> States Parties recognise the right of the child to rest and leisure, to engage in play and recreational activities appropriate to the age of the child and to participate freely in cultural life and the arts.

A Serious Case for Play and Longer Playtimes

In our current school system, children have a morning playtime, lunchtime break and if they are lucky an afternoon playtime. Pellegrini (2005) suggests more frequent breaks, such as those in Finland where students have a 15-minute outdoor free-play break every hour of every single school day (regardless of the weather) until high school.

For years now, it has been said that Finland has the best primary school system in the world. It is consistently ranked at or near the top of the Programme for International Student Assessment (PISA) list while OECD countries and the United States have seen their positions tumble. Finland leads the way in its discovery that play is the most fundamental engine and efficiency booster of children's learning.

Why Encourage Children to Play Games?

In the *Sydney Morning Herald* (2016), William Doyle interviewed Heikki Happonenen, chief of Finland's association of eight national university teacher training schools; Happonenen says 'Children's brains work better when they are moving. Not only do they concentrate better in class, but they are more successful at "negotiating, socialising, building teams and friendships together"'. Finland leads the way in its discovery that play is the most fundamental engine and efficiency booster of children's learning. The nation's children learn through play until age seven and then they are guaranteed regular playtimes throughout their day in primary school.

This fact that Finnish schools provide their students with substantially more downtime over the course of a school day can be seen to contribute, at least in part, to the fact that Finnish students are not only healthier but better learners than American and British students.

Long teaching and learning sessions are not good for anyone because we need to give our brains time to rest, which can give us a new perspective and focus. Pellegrini (2005), in his research, found that pupils were always more attentive after a break than before.

Pellegrini's research shows that 'the longer someone sits down to attend, the less attentive he is'. He adds that children are more attentive in the classroom after recess than before and that the social give-and-take of the schoolyard teaches children to work together.

Murray and Ramstetter (2013) concluded that children need to have downtime between complex cognitive challenges.

It is therefore crucial in our world today that as educators, we continue to support and value the role of play. It is also vital that we remind children to play old games and teach and encourage them to play new ones. I believe that many games are not lost, only forgotten, and that with a little help and support from us in teaching games, we will reignite the flame in our children and they will then pass these games on to the next generation.

This book has been such a joy to write and I have learnt so much. I would highly recommend playing games at home as well as at school. Amber, my daughter, and I tested out many of these games while she was at primary school and with the children in our neighbourhood. More recently, over COVID-19 and lockdown, we had immense mother-daughter fun playing games again.

Teaching playground games and running Positive Playtime projects has become one of my missions and now 20 years and hundreds of playtime projects later, it is with great delight and lots of experience that I finally get to share this book with you. To young and old alike, enjoy, have fun and play, play, play!

> We don't stop playing because we grow old, we grow old because we stop playing.
>
> *(George Bernard Shaw)*

This book and resources (as in the appendices) are intended to provide you with a toolkit of ideas to support children, lunchtime supervisors, teaching assistants, teachers, parents/carers, breakfast and after school clubs or any other adult involved with children at play in learning new games and celebrating old ones.

There are 101 games to choose from (researched and field-tested). The games are divided up into ten different sections which include:

1. Traditional playground games
2. Tag games
3. Chasing and catching games
4. Singing and dancing games
5. Skipping games and rhymes
6. Circle games
7. Parachute games
8. Quiet games
9. Co-operative games
10. Games from around the world

Each game is specifically marked with the age range, equipment and number of players required. Most of the games can be played all year long, even in the winter. If it's too cold or wet to go outside, the quiet singing and dancing games and circle games sections provide options for small spaces, halls and classrooms.

Organising a Games Session

You can discover more about a person in an hour of play than in a year of conversation.

(Plato, 429–347 BC)

When organising a games session, there are a few important considerations.

Be Creative and Flexible

There are no hard and fast rules. Feel free to change and adapt the activities and suggestions in ways that work best for you and the children. I can almost guarantee that they will come up with interesting and creative ideas and additional rules and rhymes that adults haven't even heard of.

When playing 40/40 the other day, at a school I was working with, the children told me of a new rule. Once the person had been chosen to be 'it' and before they started counting, they had to say to the rest of the players, 'Go hide and no full or near surrounding!' This meant that the children couldn't hide too close to the home base! So please give the children creative freedom and be flexible.

Terminology

Home – the base that children run back to, which can be a bench, tree, post and so on.

It, on, in and so on – one person is named as the lead player. Their responsibility is usually to chase or search for another player. They remain 'it' for a period of time and then a new player will be chosen.

Player – I have used the term 'player' instead of child, since these games are intended to be read and used by children as well as adults.

Leader – the player who leads and organises the game.

Games Per Page

There is one game per page, with all games having the same layout.

- name of game

- duration of game

- age range

- ideal number of players

- equipment needed

- how to play

- variations

- comments

In some games you will find additional information under the headings: Variations and Comments.

Photocopiable Resource

Games in this book can be photocopied. This book is intended as a resource that will support you in endless ways. I would suggest that you photocopy individual games or the various game sections of the book onto coloured card and then laminate them. For instance, with the skipping games section, photocopy the games, laminate them and create a mini-book of skipping games and keep them in your box of skipping ropes.

Many games don't require equipment, so you can start playing them with your children immediately.

The Traditional Playground Games section is a free online resource and can be downloaded from https://theresehoyle.com/free-playground-games/ and shared with family, friends and colleagues. This chapter of ten games can also be given to the playground activity leaders (PALs) and lunchtime supervisors to form part of their training programme. It will give them a bank of ten games to play at lunchtimes and playtimes.

Gender

Rather than use he/she throughout the book, which can become very cumbersome, I have used both genders equally throughout the range of games. In no way at any point do I want to suggest a stereotype in any kind of game. It is intended that you adapt the gender to the children you are working with.

Age

This book is intended to be used with primary age children from 4 to 11. The games, however, can be played by anyone, young and old!

Rules and Responsibilities for the Playground

Why Do We Need Rules?

One of the main reasons schools hire me to work with them is because of the high number of injuries and bullying at playtime. In fact, playground injuries are the leading cause of injury to children aged 5–14 in the school environment. Additionally, 75 per cent of bullying happens in the school playground (Sharp and Smith, 1991–1993). Therefore, rules that keep children physically and emotionally safe are essential. **School rules also provide clarity and consistency to all concerned.** In many schools, you will see rules, codes of conduct or values beautifully displayed inside the school buildings and classrooms, but they often forget to put them outside in the playground. If this is the case, then children learn that there is a different set of moral values inside to outside!

How to Use This Book

So, if you don't currently have rules for your outside spaces, look at your current indoor rules and adapt them for your playground.

Where to Start

I encourage schools to look at their current rules and think through with students the rules or values that need to be in place in the playground.

If you don't have clear rules in place speak to the children, staff and lunchtime supervisors and discuss the moral values and behaviours that are important to them at playtimes and lunchtimes and would make the playground and school a safe and nurturing place, where they can learn and flourish.

Get them all to draw up the rules they would like and then draw the themes together.

Rules generally fall into the following 4R categories:

- Respect for self

- Respect for others

- Respect for property and the environment

- Responsibility for all your actions

Some basic rules that I find work well at playtimes and lunchtimes are:

- We are kind and gentle

- We play safely and look after each other

- We listen to each other

- We are honest and truthful

- We take care of our school, playground and equipment

- We are respectful and polite

When you have created your school's playground rules, get a signwriter to put them onto Perspex and then display in various parts of the playground.

At the start of the academic year in the welcome back assembly, it's important to remind children of the school and playground rules. New children won't know these and other children may have forgotten in the six-week summer holidays! It is also important that every member of staff is invited to this assembly, including lunchtime supervisors, so that the children see that everyone in the school knows what the rules are and that everyone is working together.

Rules When Playing Games

All games have rules that need to be abided by and children are good at adapting and creating their own rules, often through common consent. Some basic rules that I find work well in all games are:

- Be kind

- Play fairly

- Be safe

Rewards

At playtimes, the reward is always that children get to play and have fun! There are many rewards on the market; however, over the years of running playground programmes, I have developed my own that schools love to use. You'll find these in the *101 Playground Games* online resources section (at the back of the book) and in my online website shop. Below is some information about them.

Star Player, Star Child, Caught Being Good Reward Slips

These slips are part of reward systems for you to choose between or you may choose to use them all! When children are seen playing co-operatively, being kind, letting someone join in their game and generally keeping the playground rules, they get a paper slip. These incentives can then link back into teacher's classroom rewards or children can collect their slips each week and every class can give a playground star certificate to the child or children who get the most slips. Many teachers also like to do drum roll and draw. When a child receives a slip, his name is put on it and into the drum (box). At the end of the week, there is a drum roll and five to ten slips are drawn out and those children are then awarded a prize.

Playground Star Award

This is a special certificate (see playground games online resource section) that is given out in assembly to a specific child who has kept to the rules and played well. Teachers can choose criteria for selection from week to week and ideally choose different children over the school year. It can also be given to children that received the most reward slips (see above).

How to Use This Book

Consequences

The consequence of breaking rules is that they have a verbal warning. If they then break the rule again, they are out of the game for ten minutes. Children can join in the game once they have had time out and if they can tell you the rule they need to be keeping.

If the children are organising the games, they are generally very clear with one another as to what is acceptable and what is not!

Choosing Teams

I remember cringing when I played sports. Team leaders were usually chosen by the teacher and then they had to proceed to pick their team, with them alternating in picking who they most desired! You always hoped that you wouldn't be the last person to get chosen!

Children have different ways of selecting team members and I would not advocate the above. Some possible ideas are:

- Choose teams by who has a birthday, who is wearing a certain colour, who has a certain colour hair and so on.

- Choosing teams randomly; if for instance two teams are required, numbering children off, one, two, one, two and so on.

Choosing 'It'

Some possible ideas are:

- Ask for a volunteer.

- Children have different rhymes to select who can be 'it'. One I heard the other day was 'Ip dip, sky blue, who's it, not you!' Another one was, 'Coconut, coconut, coconut crack'. On 'crack', you are out! The final one left in is then 'it'.

- Alternatively, children pick pieces of paper from a hat with 'it' written on one.

Choosing a Playground Games Activity Area

Ask the adults and children to work together on deciding where the best place would be to have a games area. It helps if the area has boundaries and is of a good size. Once decided, this remains the set games activity area for the playground and children and adults know where to congregate at playtimes when they want to play games.

You may also want to create additional zoned activity areas. In the quiet games section, I have described creating a quiet area, so that children can play quiet games and activities.

Explaining a Game

1. Read out the game to the group and explain the rules as clearly and simply as possible. Do it in a fun way, encouraging participation and playfulness.
2. Make sure that everyone can see and hear you. Stand on the edge of the circle rather than in the middle.
3. Ask if there are any questions.
4. Extend an invitation to play saying, 'let's play' rather than 'you are going to play'.
5. Always ask for a volunteer to be 'it' or choose from the ideas previously mentioned.
6. Play each game a couple of times.
7. Always look for opportunities to make a game more fun – add fantasy, chanting, singing, change the name to the latest craze and so on.
8. Encourage participation, effort and satisfaction rather than winning.
9. Ask for feedback on how it went.
10. Once there is agreement that the game is working, the responsibility for playing the game with the agreed rules and guidelines can be left with the children.

Game of the Week or Games Menu

Choose a new game to learn each week. www.routledge.com/9780367338565 – You can photocopy the game onto coloured card and then laminate it. This can be introduced in assembly and displayed in the playground so that children can learn and practise it at lunchtime. Encourage your lunchtime supervisors to get involved in playing the game of the week (GOW) with the children.

Additionally, children may like to select from a games menu, which has a selection of games to be played each week of the term.

By the end of the year, the lunchtime supervisors and children will have a toolkit of games to draw from and you'll have much happier playtimes.

Games Training for the Adults

On my How to Be a Lunchtime Supervisor Superhero and Positive Playtime courses, staff are often reluctant to play games! However, many of them tell me at the end of the games session how much fun they've had! Janna, a lunchtime supervisor, recently commented: 'I so enjoyed playing the playground games today with Thérèse Hoyle. It reminded me of all the games I used to play as a child. I feel inspired now to go outside and play these with the children'.

I would suggest that lunchtime supervisors, teachers and any other adults involved in playtimes have at least one to two hours of games training. This would be to introduce new games and reinforce and remind them of old ones.

How to Use This Book

I hear and I forget. I see and I remember. I do and I understand.

(Confucius)

As the saying goes, the best way of learning anything new is to do it!

What to do:

- Select 10–20 games from the book – Chapter 1, the traditional games chapter and a selection of other games. Copy and laminate them onto coloured card. Give one set to each member of staff. Select a leader to organise the games.

- Go play!

- Evaluate the games.

This is also a great team-building exercise and involves lots of fun!

Organising Games in the Playground – Adults and Children Playing Together

Children are drawn to activities that involve interested and interesting adults, whether those activities are highly structured or open ended.

(Elizabeth Wood, 2007)

In my experience of working in schools, the best playtimes are those that are well organised with a balance of free play and of activities children can choose to get involved in.

It is important to remember that if we are to expect children to play games in the playground, then it helps if we adults get involved too. It is also great fun! I have often found that if I have children who are well trained in the games, they can take over once I have left.

How to Get Your Lunchtime Supervisors Engaging and Playing Games with the Children

One of the main complaints I hear from headteachers is that the lunchtime staff are standing around chatting at playtimes and not engaging with the children. This may be because there isn't a clear explanation to lunchtime supervisors of their role and responsibilities, or it could be because of their lack of training and confidence.

Without a doubt, school lunchtimes can be one of the hardest times in the school day and lunchtime supervisors can have an incredibly challenging role. They are also often the least trained, lowest paid and frequently most unsupported member of staff. Therefore, it is essential if we want them to engage and play games with the children that we provide them with lunchtime supervisor training to support them in being skilled and competent. As part of this, they can either attend the whole school staff games training or have training organised specifically for them. Once your lunchtime supervisors are fully trained, they can take it in turns to organise games and support the smooth and harmonious running of any lunchtime.

Suggestions

Create a rota so that there are one or two lunchtime supervisors outside organising games and activities each playtime. The lunchtime supervisors usually work alongside the PALs.

- Join in with the games.

- Watch how the games are going and step in to make changes if necessary but keep a low profile.

- If a game becomes unsafe, step in, stop it and remind everyone of the rules and that the game is supposed to be fun.

Playground Games – Spreading the Message

Many children have lost the art of knowing how to play games and our job as adults can be to inspire and remind them. We can do this in a variety of ways.

Physical Education Lessons

I would suggest that teachers teach playground games once a term in their physical education (PE) lessons. The benefits can then be seen out in the playground. In one school I worked with, the games were played as a warm-up at the start of their PE lesson. This way, new games are regularly introduced.

I remember teaching games in my PE lessons when I was teaching in London and being thrilled to find the children playing many of the games outside. Sometimes as teachers we aren't sure if children will transfer their in-school learning to outside! It's refreshing when they do!

Assemblies

In primary schools, assemblies take place on most days of the week. I would suggest that once a week, preferably on a Monday morning, part of the assembly is dedicated to 'Playground News' and on Fridays, awards can be given out for good play. Introduce:

- the game of the week (GOW)

- remind children of the rules for games and the playground

- playground PALs and any exciting news from them

- where the games will be happening

- children who have news or new games they would like to share

Playground Activity Leaders (PALs)

PALs consist of a group of Year 5 or 6 children whose main role is to encourage and organise games in the games activity area during playtimes and the lunch break and help make the playground a safer, more enjoyable space for younger children.

These pupils take on a leadership role at playtimes and lunchtimes, form part of the playtime council and are identifiable by the cap or tabard they wear.

When considering adopting this system in your school, please give consideration to the following:

- How many PALs do you need, given the size of your playground and number of children in your school?

- How many times a week would be suitable for them to be out on games duty?

- How would the PALs be chosen?

- What support will they need?

Recruiting and Interviewing Your PALs

When introducing the idea/concept of PALs to staff and children, I encourage school leaders to host an assembly explaining the role of the PAL, what they will be expected to do, the qualities they will need and how to become a PAL. The school leader then explains that Year 5 and 6 will be given application forms and will be shown how to fill them out if they would like to apply (see a template in the resources section). I also encourage school leaders to create a recruitment campaign where children can design and display attractive posters saying 'Wanted, Playground Activity Leaders, Apply Now!'

Once the children have completed the application form, a date is set for interviews; this is preferably with a senior manager, teaching assistant, teacher, lunchtime supervisor and someone from the community. Some schools I have worked with have managed to get the local Tesco or Co-op manager and one school I know managed to get a famous local football player! So be as creative as you like with the interview team!

I've often found in the recruitment and interviewing stage I've had huge numbers apply. I believe there are many reasons for this including good marketing and promotion, talking with the children about what the role would involve and creating excitement about being a PAL and a school leader.

Once your leaders have been selected, create two groups A and B. A group are on for three days and B group for two days. Whatever you do, do not have them working all week, they will lose motivation and need to have some free playtime of their own.

Responsibilities of the PALs

Its important PALs understand their responsibilities and what's expected of them.

Their responsibilities will be dependent on the size, demographics, ethos and the playtime management of each school. However, these are some things they can be responsible for:

- Organising games

- Looking after younger children

- Spotting children at the friendship stop and finding them a friend to play with or getting them involved in a game

- Taking out and putting away playground equipment

- Mediation (this involves additional training and is a skilled role)

PALs Support Coach

Ideally all members of the playground PALs meet regularly with an assigned adult responsible for PALs training, ongoing support and supervision (PALs coach). This is usually a teaching assistant, lunchtime supervisor or teacher.

Many reasons the PALs system fails is because these children are expected to get on with their role by themselves, without any training or supervision.

How to Use This Book

Training the PALs to Teach the Games

Step 1   –   Discuss roles and responsibilities, rules for themselves, playground rules, rotas, period of time that they are elected to be a PAL (weekly, half-term or full-term) and so on.

Step 2   –   Introduce a selection of games and remind the children of games they already know. I suggest that you copy the Traditional Playground Games section of the book and give each PAL a pack of games that they can keep and use as a reference. This will give them ten playground games to learn and introduce to other children.

Step3   –   The PALs plan and organise a game to play with younger children.

Step 4   –   The PALs evaluate how the game went and continue to learn new games.

Step 5   –   The PALs choose a uniform that distinguishes them in the playground, this may be a baseball cap, tabard, badge and so on.

Step 6   –   A rota is agreed.

Step 7   –   The PALs are introduced in assembly to all of the school.

Step 8   –   The PALs, on their assigned days, go out and play games in the playground with the children.

Step 9   –   The PALs contribute to Playground News at assemblies.

Step 10   –   The PALs meet weekly with the assigned adults who support them.

Games Rota

Create a rota for adults and PALs who are to play games with the children each day. Ideally, the PALs are only on duty two or three times a week.

Ongoing Support

The PALs need to have a regular time to talk about their experiences, the successes and the challenges with their coach. Ideally this meeting is weekly. The PALs should be known to all staff so that they can give support and encouragement. Their parents/carers can also be informed.

At the end of six weeks or the end of term, the PALs should receive a certificate to thank them for their contribution and hard work. This is given out in assembly.

I do hope you have lots of fun setting up and organising your games sessions. Let us remember, play has great value not only for the children, but for us adults too – enjoy and go play!

Children have a full time occupation. It's called PLAY. Let them be occupied by it from their early years until their twilight years.

(Vince Gowmon)

1. Farmer, Farmer, May We Cross Your Golden River?
2. In and Out the Dusty Bluebells
3. What's the Time Mr Wolf?
4. Grandmother's Footsteps
5. Fishes in the Sea
6. Duck, Duck, Goose
7. Captain's Coming
8. The Keeper of the Treasure
9. I Sent a Letter to My Love
10. Mother May I?

Traditional Playground Games

Play is an essential part of the development of all children and traditional playground games have been played for hundreds of years all over the world.

Once a child reaches school age and begins to play with other children, play becomes a social occasion and games become elaborate rituals.

When playing traditional games, children have an incredible capacity to be poetic and creative. In contrast to when they are taught games in PE where the rules are fixed, in the playground they can influence how games are played. You may notice children's love of rhymes with these old traditional games. I have found that these are often adapted and can exist for the pleasure of themselves and to help children to make sense of the world and reflect cultural fears. I remember the rhyme, 'My mother said, I never should, play with gypsies in the wood'; this reflected some of our cultural fears at the time. In and Out the Dusty Blue Bells used to have the ending, 'You will be my master'. Most children now say, 'You will be my partner'. This reflects the passage of time and more cultural and ethical awareness and sensitivity. While listening to children playing, you may also have heard some rhymes verging on the taboo!

In the playground, children have the freedom to be themselves, unencumbered by the rules and regulations of us adults. There is what Opie and Opie (1969) call a 'juvenile code'.

When it comes to rules, children often have their own for games or they find ways to make them more co-operative and fair or just more fun!

A few years ago I played the game, Duck, Duck, Goose with a group of children. They had made up different rules that made the game even better and I have included their ideas in this game. When the goose was caught by the trapper, he reverted to being a duckling and had to squat down in the centre of the inner circle and make duck-like noises and gestures with his arms. This child remained in the centre of the circle until another duck was caught.

Traditional Games in This Section

I have chosen many popular games that children regularly play in the playground and games that I loved to play in my childhood for this section of *101 Playground Games*.

Game number seven, Captain's Coming, used to be a favourite game of mine at Brownies and is still frequently played by Guide, Cub and Scout groups.

Grandmother's Footsteps is a popular game throughout the world and was another favourite of mine. I have chosen to call it the name that we used. In many books you will see it referred to as Statues or Red Light, Green Light. You will find that some games have alternative names and the children may want to re-name or adapt them. Do add their ideas and suggestions when you photocopy the games and please email me new games and any suggestions that make these games even better.

Traditional playground games and games in general have, over the years, been handed down from generation to generation. Many of these games were played in playgrounds, streets, playing fields and the countryside, in my childhood. However, sadly many of our children do not have the freedom of these open spaces with fears of stranger danger and busy roads. In addition, our children are spending ever-increasing amounts of time inside playing games on screens and watching TV, which inevitably means they are getting less and less time to play.

I feel very strongly that part of my legacy is to pass on these traditional games so that the children I work with can then teach them to the next generation. Please help me by teaching these traditional games to your children, so that we can all leave a legacy.

If you have any additional games you would like to add to my collection, please email me at therese@theresehoyle.com

1. Farmer, Farmer, May We Cross Your Golden River?

Time: 15 minutes
Age Range: 6–10
Ideal Number of Players: 6+
Equipment Needed: None

How to Play

One player is named the farmer and stands in the middle of a designated area of the playground.

The other players stand behind a line, in a row about ten metres away from the farmer.

A designated 'home' area is agreed, usually the opposite end of the play area.

The players call out, 'Farmer, Farmer, may we cross your golden river?'

The farmer replies, 'Not unless you have the colour … on'.

Those players lucky enough to have that colour on may cross the playground safely to the designated home area.

The farmer then counts to five, and on five the other players must walk or run 'home' while the farmer tries to catch them. Anyone who is caught helps the farmer to choose what colour the players should be wearing next to be able to cross the river.

The game continues with a different colour each time until the last player is caught and she becomes the farmer.

Variations

Once a player is caught, they stand in the middle, join hands with the farmer and help him catch other players.

Comments

Make sure all players keep inside the marked area.

2. In and Out the Dusty Bluebells

Time: 10–15 minutes
Age Range: 4–9
Ideal Number of Players: 8+
Equipment Needed: None

How to Play

> In and out the dusty bluebells
> In and out the dusty bluebells
> In and out the dusty bluebells
> Who shall be my partner?
>
> Tippity, tappity on your shoulders
> Tippity, tappity on your shoulders
> Tippity, tappity on your shoulders
> You shall be my partner.

This is a ring dance for at least eight dancers.

Verse 1

Everyone stands in a circle holding their hands up high to make an arch between each dancer. One dancer is chosen and skips in and out of the arches while all players sing the rhyme.

Verse 2

On 'Who shall be my partner?' the dancer stops and taps whoever is closest on the shoulder. This dancer then joins on to the first dancer and they weave in and out again as the first verse is repeated. The game is repeated until all the children form a chain, then they all skip around for as long as they like.

3. What's the Time Mr Wolf?

Time: 20 minutes
Age Range: 5–11
Ideal Number of Players: 12–20
Equipment Needed: None

How to Play

One player is chosen to be Mr Wolf.

The other players stand in a line at the opposite end of the playground about 10–12 metres away from Mr Wolf. This line is referred to as 'home'.

Mr Wolf stands with his back to them.

The players chant, 'What's the time Mr Wolf?'

Mr Wolf replies (for example), '3 o'clock'.

The players advance the same number of steps, that is, three steps for 3 o'clock.

The game continues until Mr Wolf thinks the players are close enough to catch and after being asked the time again he replies, 'Dinner time', then turns and chases the players. The first child caught becomes Mr Wolf.

If Mr Wolf does not catch anyone, he has to be Mr Wolf again.

If a player reaches Mr Wolf before dinnertime, they tap Mr Wolf on the shoulder and run for home. If the player gets home, then she is safe. If she is caught, then she becomes Mr Wolf.

Variations

In some versions of this, when Mr Wolf catches a player they have to return to home.

4. Grandmother's Footsteps

Time: 15 minutes
Age Range: 5–11
Ideal Number of Players: 6+
Equipment Needed: None

How to Play

Players stand at a 'home' base in a line.

Grandmother stands with her back to them about ten metres away.

The players creep forward, but whenever Grandmother whirls round they must stop advancing and freeze'.

If she sees any of them moving, she sends them back to the starting line again.

The child who is the first to touch Grandmother becomes the next Grandmother.

Variations

Before Grandmother can turn around, she must count to ten or say a rhyme such as, 'L-o-n-d-o-n spells London' or 'one, two, three, four, five jam tarts'.

She can say this quietly, under her breath, so the other players can't hear and don't know when Grandmother is about to turn around.

Comments

This game is also called Sly Fox, Peep behind the Curtain or Black Pudding.

5. Fishes in the Sea

Time: 10–15 minutes
Age Range: 5–10
Ideal Number of Players: 8+
Equipment Needed: None

How to Play

The players stand in a circle. They are alternately named cod, salmon, plaice and haddock.

One player is chosen to be the Fisherman. This person is the caller and stands in the middle of the circle.

When a fish name is called, all the players in that category move around the outside of the circle in a clockwise direction until they reach their places again. They are instructed on how to move with various directions. For example, cod – high tide; salmon – coral reef; plaice – tide turns and so on.

High tide – move quickly.

Low tide – move slowly.

Tide turns – change direction.

Fisherman about – crouch down low to avoid the nets.

Sharks – walk backwards.

Coral reef – jump.

The last person back to their place becomes the Fisherman.

6. Duck, Duck, Goose

Time: 10–15 minutes
Age Range: 6–10
Ideal Number of Players: 10+
Equipment Needed: None

How to Play

The players sit in a large circle facing inwards.

One player is chosen to be the 'tapper' and walks around the outside of the circle. As he walks around, he touches each child gently on the head while saying, 'duck, duck, duck'.

At some stage he will tap a child and say, 'goose', instead.

The goose then jumps up and chases the tapper around the circle.

The tapper in turn tries to get all the way back to the goose's spot, 'home', without getting caught.

If the tapper gets home safely, the goose becomes the new tapper and the game starts again.

If the goose catches the tapper, the game starts again with the tapper being on again.

Variations

When the goose gets caught by the tapper, he then reverts to being a duckling and has to squat down in the centre of the inner circle and make duck-like noises and gestures with his arms. This player then remains in the centre of the circle until another goose is caught.

Comments

If the person who has been picked as the goose manages to get back to the space first, they can then fold their arms so they are not chosen again.

7. Captain's Coming

Time: 10–15 minutes
Age Range: 5–11
Ideal Number of Players: 6+
Equipment Needed: None

How to Play

The players assemble in the centre of the playground or in a hall. A leader is chosen who calls out various commands. The commands need explanation to each participant before the game can begin. A game of Captain's Coming can have any number of various commands; the more there are, the more that needs to be memorised, and the harder it is to play.

The group competes with each other to complete the commands. If there is an obvious person or, if applicable, group of people who are last to start a command, they are then out. The game continues until there is only one person left – the winner.

The Commands

Bow – everyone races to the front of the room.

Stern – everyone races to the back of the room.

Starboard – everyone races to the right of the room.

Port – everyone races to the left of the room.

Captain's coming – everyone stands tall, salutes and shouts, 'Aye aye Captain'.

Captain's wife – everyone curtseys.

Scrub the decks – mime scrubbing on hands and knees.

Climb the rigging – everyone pretends to climb a rope ladder.

Man the lifeboat – find a partner and hold both hands. Anyone without a partner is out.

Sharks – lie on back with feet up.

Freeze – stop all actions when this is called. If a further command is given without saying 'unfreeze', anyone obeying it is out.

Variations

There are lots of variations of this game. You can find many alternatives by doing a Google search of Captain's Coming on the internet or you may want to make up your own. To make this a more co-operative game, you can just play for the fun with nobody being out.

Comments

This game is also a good wet play game.

8. The Keeper of the Treasure

Time: 10–25 minutes
Age Range: 4–10
Ideal Number of Players: 8–30
Equipment Needed: Keys or a bean bag

How to Play

A suitable treasure is found (a bean bag, set of keys).

· The players form a circle and create a space large enough to represent a door for the children to run through.

A leader is chosen.

One player is chosen to be the keeper of the treasure. She then sits in the middle of the circle with her eyes closed and the treasure placed behind her back.

The leader then silently selects a robber by pointing to a player.

The robber then tiptoes as quietly as possible up to the keeper and steals the treasure from behind the keeper's back.

Once the keeper realises the robber has the treasure, she leaps to her feet and chases the robber, in a clockwise direction, around the circle, with the intent of catching him. The aim of the game is either for the keeper to catch the robber or for the robber to get back to the keeper's home base in the centre of the circle.

While the players wait for the robber to steal the treasure, they chant, 'The robber is coming, the robber is coming, the robber is coming', and then as the robber picks up the treasure and runs out of the door they shout, 'The robber has come!'

If the keeper catches the robber, then she is the keeper again and a new robber is chosen. If the robber gets back to the home base in the centre, then he is safe and becomes the keeper and a new robber is chosen.

Comments

If you find when playing this game that players run through gaps in the circle other than the door, it may be helpful at the start of the game to create a rule which says players cannot jump/run out of the windows (the gaps), they can only run out of the door.

9. I Sent a Letter to My Love

Time: 10–20 minutes
Age Range: 4–11
Ideal Number of Players: 6–20+
Equipment Needed: An item to use as the letter, an envelope, a handkerchief, hat, glove, beanbag or similar item

How to Play

Everyone forms a circle, standing or sitting. One player with a letter (the item) walks or skips around the outside of the circle as the rhyme is chanted.

> I sent a letter to my love,
> And on the way I dropped it.
> Someone must have picked it up,
> And put it in their pocket.
> It wasn't you; it wasn't you,
> It was you!

As the player says, 'It wasn't you', he gently taps each player in the circle on the shoulder and repeats, 'It wasn't you', as many times as he likes with him finally saying, 'It was you!' and dropping the letter on the ground behind the player.

On 'you', the player who has the letter picks it up and chases the 'letter dropper' around the circle with the aim of catching him.

If the letter dropper gets back into the chaser's place without being caught, then he is safe and the other player becomes the letter dropper. If she catches the letter dropper, he is on again and the game starts again.

The players continue singing the rhyme.

The last one back is the new letter dropper.

Variations

You can substitute 'I sent a letter to my love' with 'I sent a letter to my friend'.

10. Mother May I?

Time: 10–15 minutes
Age Range: 4–11
Ideal Number of Players: 6+
Equipment Needed: None

How to Play

One player is 'Mother'.

The other players line up and face Mother about ten metres away.

Mother selects one of the players and says something like, '(name of player), you may take five giant steps'. That player then responds with, 'Mother, may I?' Mother replies, 'Yes, you may'.

Mother then addresses another player and the game continues until one of the children reaches Mother. Whoever makes it to Mother first becomes Mother for the next round.

Does this sound simple? It is! Except that in the excitement of the game, someone is bound to take their steps without asking 'Mother, may I?' When that happens, Mother reminds the player of her manners and the player is sent back to the beginning of the line.

Variations

Here are some ideas for the different ways children can move.

Scissors step – jump while crossing your feet, then jump while uncrossing them.

Banana step – lying down with feet at current spot, marking where the top of your head was and getting up there for a new spot.

Bunny hop – a hop.

Baby steps – small steps.

Giant strides – giant steps.

For an older children's variation, try this one: 'Fourth cousin once removed on my father's side, may I?'

Tag Games

Tag Games

Tag

In games of Tag (also known as It, Had, He, Tips, Tig, Touch, Tab, Tiggy, Tick, Dobby, Chasing, Chasemaster, Chasey and other names), the object is to tag, or touch, other players who are then out of the game. Usually, one player is 'it' and has to chase and tag the other players, one of whom then becomes the new person who is 'it'.

Tag is played throughout the world and is a simple game. Most forms require neither teams, nor scores nor sports equipment such as balls, but it may be made more complex with various rule modifications. Both of these aspects make Tag a popular game amongst children and it is often played in informal areas such as playgrounds or backyards.

Rules

The rules of Tag are very flexible. Rules such as the following can be either decided before the game or added as the game progresses to make play fairer.

At the beginning of the game, one player is designated 'it'. After 'it' is chosen, the other players scatter. 'It' must chase them and tag them, usually by tapping them somewhere on the body. A tagged player becomes 'it' and the former 'it' joins the others in trying to avoid being tagged. This process repeats until the game ends.

In a typical game of Tag, no score is kept nor is a winner selected. Those who can avoid being tagged or who can stay 'it' for the least amount of time are generally regarded as the best players. There is usually no time limit; the end of the game is chosen arbitrarily, perhaps when the players tire of the game, when playtime ends or when players get called home for dinner.

Borders

In order to keep the action fast and fun, a game of Tag often has arbitrary borders that the players cannot step beyond, such as a fenced-in school playground, netball court, garden or field. This prevents players from running far beyond the area where the game started, to avoid being tagged, and keeps all the players in close vicinity to give the 'it' a better chance of tagging somebody.

A game of Tag may also have one or more 'bases', usually a landmark such as a bench, pole, fence, tree trunk or section of wall. When a base is touched or stood upon, it grants a player exemption from being tagged. 'Base' is sometimes called 'Safe', 'Home', 'Bar', 'Tee', 'Den' or 'Homie'.

No Tag Backs

'No tag backs' (also 'can't get the butcher back', 'zap-zap no tap back', 'no master backs', 'no catch backs', 'no tap backs', 'no returns' or 'no touchbacks'), is a phrase that can be used in most Tag variants. If the person who is 'it' tags another player, and then the player tries to tag the person back, the former 'it' player can say, 'No tag backs'. This means that the person who is 'it' can't immediately tag the person who made them 'it'. This rule was created to allow the former 'it' player not only a chance to get out of close proximity of the current 'it' player, but to give them a few moments of immunity to catch their breath. Whether or not 'tag backs' are allowed in the ensuing game must be established at the start of the game to ensure fairness of play for all players.

Babysitting

A player who is 'it' who hovers around base, waiting for players to leave or get on, is said to be 'babysitting' (also 'baby lining', 'coast guarding', 'puppy guarding', 'doggy guarding', 'monkey guarding', 'bodyguarding', 'chicken guarding', 'goose guarding', 'coffin guarding', 'den hanging', 'laying eggs' or 'camping'; in England, 'post hanging' or 'doggy watching'; in Scotland; 'den poaching'). If a player is unable to leave base because of the imminent threat of being tagged, the player on base can say, 'No babysitting!' meaning the person who is 'it' can't trap the player on the base. If 'no babysitting' is said, the person who is 'it' should move away to give the other player a chance to move off the base.

11. Circle Tag

Time: 10 minutes
Age Range: 6–10
Ideal Number of Players: 12+
Equipment Needed: None

How to Play

Mark a large circle on the playground using chalk or use existing playground markings.

Select three or four players to be 'it'. You may want them to wear sashes or bibs.

The other players run around an identified playing area.

When tagged, the player goes and stands in the circle.

The circle can be guarded by one of the players wearing a sash. This person is called the 'guard'.

The other 'free' children can free the 'captured' children in the circle by tapping their hand, as long as they themselves are not tagged by the guard.

The game can be stopped after 30–60 seconds with new children chosen to be 'it' and the captured children being freed.

12. Sing a Song of Sixpence Tag

Time: 10–25 minutes
Age Range: 5–11
Ideal Number of Players: 8+
Equipment Needed: None

How to Play

In each corner of a defined playing area (playground/field/netball court), there are four homes for the king, the queen, the maid and the blackbird. Each player wears a different coloured sash/ribbon so that they can be distinguished. The rest of the players mime the actions as they sing the nursery rhyme 'Sing a Song of Sixpence'. When it comes to the word 'nose', they shout this in a loud voice and the four players rush out of their respective homes, with the aim of tagging another player and bringing them home. The first four tagged become the next king, queen, maid and blackbird respectively, until each player has had a turn at one of the roles.

Sing a song of sixpence,
A pocket full of sky.
Four and twenty blackbirds,
Learning how to fly.
Early in the morning,
The birds began to sing.
Wasn't that a special way
Of waking up the King?

The King was in his counting house,
Giving gifts of money.
The Queen was in the parlour,
Eating bread and honey.
The maid was in the garden,
Hanging out the clothes.
When down came a blackbird,
And kissed her on her nose!

Adapted from Positively Mother Goose *– Loomans, Kolberg and Loomans (1991).*

Comments

This can of course be sung with the traditional version of 'Sing a Song of Sixpence', though I do find this version a lot more positive!

13. Immunity Tag

Time: 10 minutes
Age Range: 5–11
Ideal Number of Players: 8+
Equipment Needed: None

How to Play

One person is chosen to be 'it'.

Some optional rules for the other players are that you are safe from being tagged if:

- you are off the ground (but may only stay for a count of ten)

- you are touching a certain agreed colour

- you are hugging another person

- you form a group of, e.g., four

- you are touching wood or iron

If you get caught by 'it' then you become the new 'it' and the game starts again.

Comments

This can be a very fast game so vary the rules to keep it interesting.

14. Stuck in the Mud

Time: 10–15 minutes
Age Range: 5–11
Ideal Number of Players: 8+
Equipment Needed: None

How to Play

One person is 'it' and chases others in the group. When they catch or touch someone, that person is frozen in place. They cannot move and must stand with their feet apart and arms stretched sideways.

They can be freed by another person crawling under their legs.

Play continues and the chaser tries to get all the players who are frozen or stuck in the mud.

The last person to be frozen is 'it' for the next game.

Variations

The larger the group, the more chasers can be 'on'.

Comments

Large groups may need a rule to encourage a one-way system when children go under the legs, for instance, back to front only, so as not to crack heads!

15. Chain Tag

Time: 10–15 minutes
Age Range: 6–11
Ideal Number of Players: 10+
Equipment Needed: None

How to Play

One player is 'it'. When a player is tagged by 'it', the two players hold hands and become 'it' together. They run holding hands, trying to tag other players.

Each time a player is tagged, she joins the 'it' chain, but only the two players on the end of the chain can tag the other players.

The chain can be as long as the children want, or they can break it into two parts when it becomes four players long. These pairs are then 'it'. The game moves along very quickly the more 'it' pairs you have.

The game ends when all players are tagged.

Variations

Instead of running, the players may choose to hop, skip, jump or choose whatever movement they like.

16. It

Time: 10–15 minutes
Age Range: 5–11
Ideal Number of Players: 6+
Equipment Needed: None

How to Play

The person who is 'it' has to run after the other children and try and touch them. If you are touched by 'it', then you become 'it'.

There are two main rules:

1. 'It' must not run after the same person all the time.
2. If you are caught by 'it', you cannot try to catch that person (who was 'it') straight away.

Variations

In one version of this game, you can call a short truce. This happens when someone being chased crosses their fingers and shouts 'kings'. This means that you cannot be caught, but it's not fair to call 'kings' every time you are on the point of being caught!

Comments

This game is also known as Touch, Tag or Catch.

17. Toilet Tag

Time: 10 minutes
Age Range: 6–11
Ideal Number of Players: 6–12
Equipment Needed: None

How to Play

One person is chosen to be the tagger/'it'. The objective of the game is to tag as many people as possible.

When the tagger tags a player, the tagged player has to freeze as if they are sitting on the toilet!

To 'free' the player, another person has to pull the tagged player's chain (players decide in advance how they are going to do this).

The aim of the game is for all players to get tagged, although this rarely happens.

Variations

It is rare in today's world to have toilet chains. An alternative option is for players to pretend to press a button on the 'tagged toilet' so that the player is then released and free!

18. Tag the Tail

Time: 10–20 minutes
Age Range: 4–11
Ideal Number of Players: 20+
Equipment Needed: Ribbon or string

How to Play

One player is chosen to be 'it'.

Every other player is given a piece of ribbon or string (the tail) that they can tuck into the back of their clothing.

If players are wearing dresses or can't tuck the tail into their clothing, have them tape their tail to their backs.

The person who is 'it' attempts to capture the tails of the players.

If 'it' tries to capture your tail, you dodge and turn so that she can't get it!

Once 'it' does capture a tail, that player then also become 'it' and joins in with the chasing and capturing of players and their tails.

The game ends when everyone's tails have been taken.

Variations

Team tag the tail. Players get into groups of five or six. Players hold each other around the waist. The last member of each team has a small piece of material tucked into the back of his clothing. The heads (front players) have to try to catch their team's tail.

19. Hospital Tag

Time: 10–15 minutes
Age Range: 6–11
Ideal Number of Players: 10+
Equipment Needed: None

How to Play

Choose someone to be 'it'.

The person who is 'it' chases everyone, attempting to tag them.

Anyone who gets tagged must hold onto the part of their body where they were touched.

Whoever is first to be tagged three times then becomes 'it'.

20. Fox and Geese

Time: 10–20 minutes
Age Range: 6–10
Ideal Number of Players: 5–8
Equipment Needed: none

How to Play

One person is the fox and stands at the front.

The remaining players make a line, facing the front.

They stand one behind the other and hold onto the waist of the person in front.

The last person in the line is the goose.

The fox tries to tag the goose.

The others move together to try to protect the goose.

If tagged, the goose becomes the new fox.

The new fox moves to the front of the line and the old fox stands behind her with everyone else moving back one place.

The new goose is the person at the end of the line and the game continues.

3 Chasing and Catching Games

Chasing and Catching Games

Chasing and catching games are similar to tag games. The games differ, however, in that they generally have a theme, a storyline or rhyme to go with them, such as cat and mouse, sharks, mother hen and so on.

These chasing and catching games have been selected because they are great fun and have produced much merriment when researching the best games to play. Poison and Seaweed were chosen because they were two of my daughter's favourite games and are the games I frequently play on my Positive Playtime and How to Be a Lunchtime Supervisor Superhero courses!

Hide and Seek is a well-loved game which I have slotted into chasing and catching because it goes so well with 40/40. It is a game that is popular the world over. I was saddened to find research from The Play England study (2008), which shows that only 6% of children in the United Kingdom named playing Hide and Seek as their favourite pastime. Instead, their favourite pastime was socialising.

I do hope that this section inspires games like Hide and Seek to be played again.

21. Poison

Time: 10–15 minutes
Age Range: 6–10
Ideal Number of Players: 5–15
Equipment Needed: Just lots of space

How to Play

One person is 'it'. They stand holding out their hand with their fingers stretched out and palms down.

Everyone else holds on lightly to 'its' fingers or thumb. Usually players stretch out as far as possible, so that they are ready to run away.

'It' then proceeds to say, 'I went to the shops to buy some…' and then says something usually beginning with 'p' such as pottery, plants and so on.

When 'it' says, 'Poison!' the players let go and run as fast as they can while 'it' tries to chase and catch one of them.

The first person caught becomes the next 'it'.

The people being chased must not let go of the chaser's fingers or start to run until they hear 'Poison!' If they do, then they must be 'it'.

Variations

In some variations of this game, there is a home base or safe area where if players reach it they cannot be caught.

With some playgrounds, there is a need to agree on a given area where players can run; if they go out of this area, they become 'it'.

Comments

This game is also known as Bingo, Release Touch or Sticky Glue.

22. Cat and Mouse

Time: 10–15 minutes
Age Range: 6–12
Ideal Number of Players: 8+
Equipment Needed: None

How to Play

Everyone stands in a circle holding hands.

One person is chosen to be the mouse. They stand inside the circle.

One person is chosen to be the cat. They stand outside the circle.

The aim of the game is for the cat to catch the mouse.

The cat tries to catch the mouse by dodging in and out of the circle.

The players have to hold hands firmly and try to stop the cat getting into the circle to catch the mouse.

If the cat does get into the circle, players must let the mouse out as quickly as possible and then try to keep the cat inside the circle.

If the cat catches the mouse, new players are then chosen to be the cat and the mouse and the game continues.

Alternatively, when the cat catches the mouse they can then become the mouse and only a new cat needs to be chosen.

Variations

If the cat is finding it difficult to catch the mouse, the group must count up to seven and allow the cat into the circle or out of the circle after the mouse. Remind the group that once the cat's head is in the circle then she is allowed through.

This is also a good parachute game (see Chapter 7 for more parachute games).

Comments

Sometimes this game needs supervising since children can become a bit rough. It is important to think through the rules needed prior to playing this game and reinforce again if this happens, for example, 'we are kind and gentle' or 'we move safely'.

23. Sharks

Time: 10–15 minutes
Age Range: 6–11
Ideal Number of Players: 12+
Equipment Needed: None

How to Play

Agree on the area of the playground to be used. Mark a box with good space to move around in.

Choose one shark.

The other players get into groups of three.

Two players hold hands facing each other and create an arch. The third player who is the fish stands in the centre of these two and the pair lower the arch with the idea of protecting the fish.

When the shark calls the word 'food', all the fish (children in the centre of the two players) have to leave their home and find a new centre. (The two players should raise their arms into an arch then drop them down onto their new 'fish'.)

The shark tries to catch a fish and if caught, the fish becomes the new shark.

The new shark counts to three and then calls 'food'; and the game continues.

Comments

Players need to change frequently from static to active roles.

24. Pop Stars

Time: 10–15 minutes
Age Range: 5–11
Ideal Number of Players: 6+
Equipment Needed: None

How to Play

One person is the leader and stands on one side of a designated area, while the other players stand facing the leader about 20 metres away.

The game leader calls out the initials of a pop star.

As soon as players think they know who the initials stand for, they race to the front and back again and call out the name.

If the player is correct with the guess, they become the next leader and the game starts again.

25. Hide and Seek

Time: 10–15 minutes
Age Range: 5–11
Ideal Number of Players: 6+
Equipment Needed: None

How to Play

A player is first chosen to be 'it' (the person who is the seeker).

He turns around and counts to 20 with his eyes closed while the rest of the players hide.

Then 'it' says, 'Ready or not, here I come', and rushes to find everyone.

The objective of the game is not to get found by 'it'.

When you are found, you are out and gather in a specific spot, which can be labelled 'home'.

Those who can remain hidden the longest are considered the best players.

Comments

Numerous variants of the game occur worldwide.

26. 40/40

Time: 10–15 minutes
Age Range: 6–11
Ideal Number of Players: 6+
Equipment Needed: None

How to Play

This game is similar to Hide and Seek except that the player who is 'it' has a base (such as a tree or post) to which the other players must return, ideally without being caught.

Firstly, choose someone to be 'it'. They count to 40 while everyone else goes away and hides.

If 'it' sees a player who is hiding or coming out of hiding they touch the home base and shout, '40/40 I see (name of the person they've just seen)' before that player reaches the base.

If they name that person, then they are 'out' and remain at the home base.

The only way the players can save themselves is to get to the home base first and shout, '40/40 home'.

The children can also run to the base and say, '40/40 save all', which means that all the caught players are free and the game starts again.

If the person who is 'it' catches everyone, then the person who was 'out' first will now be 'it' and the game continues.

27. Mother Hen

Time: 10–15 minutes
Age Range: 5–11
Ideal Number of Players: 8+
Equipment Needed: None

How to Play

Mother hen stands at one end of the 'field'.

Her chicks stand at the opposite end of the field.

The fox stands at one side, halfway between mother hen and her chicks.

Mother hen says, 'Come home, my chicks'. The chicks say, 'We're afraid the old fox will get us'. Mother hen says, 'Come home'.

The chicks must run immediately with the aim of reaching the other end of the field, where mother hen waits.

The aim of the game is for the fox to tag the chicks and put them in his den.

The game continues until all chicks are caught.

The first chick caught becomes the new fox and the last becomes mother hen.

Comments

The field can be any designated playground space which has borders, such as a netball pitch, school field, garden and so on.

28. Colours

Time: 10–15 minutes
Age Range: 5–11
Ideal Number of Players: 6+
Equipment Needed: None

How to Play

Players stand in a line facing the leader.

The leader stands at the other end of a marked space and calls a colour.

Everyone wearing that colour takes one step forward and then stands still.

Then another colour is called.

The first to touch the leader is the winner and becomes the new leader and the game starts again.

Variations

Children stand in a line facing the leader who calls out letters of the alphabet. If the child has that letter in their name, they take one step forward. The first to touch the leader is the winner.

29. Handshake

Time: 10–15 minutes
Age Range: 5–11
Ideal Number of Players: 6+
Equipment Needed: None

How to Play

Players stand in a circle.

One of the players is 'it'.

Those in the circle face inwards with their hands behind their backs.

The player who is 'it' runs around the outside of the circle, taps the hands of one of the players and carries on running.

The player whose hands were tapped runs around the circle in the opposite direction.

When they meet, they shake hands and then race back to the vacant space.

The one who gets there last is 'it' for the next round.

30. Seaweed

Time: 10–15 minutes
Age Range: 5–11
Ideal Number of Players: 10–25
Equipment Needed: None

How to Play

This tag game is played with defined boundaries – usually a large rectangular playing area about the size of one-third of a netball court. Cones can mark the area if there are no lines.

The playing area is the ocean.

All players (fish) line up on one side of the ocean.

One player is chosen to be the octopus (tagger). When the leader blows the whistle (or says, 'Go!'), the fish swim as fast as they can to the other side of the ocean where they are safe.

They must try not to get tagged by the octopus before reaching the other shore. This is repeated until the fish are narrowed to one.

If a fish gets tagged, he becomes seaweed. This means his feet must remain planted on the spot where he was tagged. When a player becomes seaweed, he becomes a friend to the octopus and can help the octopus to tag fish (without moving his feet) as they swim by.

The seaweed may not lift his roots out of the sand. If this happens, that player becomes dried up seaweed on the shore until the next game.

The last fish left in the sea becomes the octopus for the next game.

Variations

Use two or three taggers instead of one.

4 Singing and Dancing Games

Singing and Dancing Games

Singing and Dancing Games

These singing and dancing games are mainly for young children, although in a mixed-age group you will usually find some of the older children joining in and enjoying the games too. The Hokey Cokey is the exception that can be played by any age child or adult!

These games are sometimes referred to as ring games and are all accompanied by familiar songs and rhymes. Ring a Ring o' Roses is the simplest of all these games and can be played by even the smallest children.

Many of these games have historical significance, with Ring a Ring o' Roses being attributed to the Black Death/plague of the 14th century: the 'ring o' roses' was the red rash shaped in a ring which was a symptom of the plague, the 'pocket full o' posies' were the herbs that people carried in an attempt to ward off the disease, 'Atishoo!' was the flu-like symptoms and 'we all fall down' meant you were dead!

The origins of the rhyme Pop Goes the Weasel are believed to date back to the 1700s.

The words are derived from Cockney rhyming slang, which originated in London. Cockneys were a close community and had a suspicion of strangers and a dislike of the police. They developed a language of their own based roughly on rhyming slang. It was difficult for strangers to understand as invariably the second noun would always be dropped. Apples and pears (meaning stairs) would be abbreviated to just 'apples', for instance, 'Watch your step on the apples'. To 'pop' is the slang word for 'pawn'. Weasel is derived from 'weasel and stoat' meaning coat. It was traditional for even poor people to own a suit, which they wore as their 'Sunday best'. When times were hard, they would pawn their suit, or coat, on a Monday and claim it back before Sunday. Hence the term 'pop goes the weasel'.

Oranges and Lemons is a very old game and rhyme which has been very loved by numerous generations of children all over the world. The rhyme refers to bells around central London – St Clement's, St Martin's-in-the-Field, the Old Bailey and St Mary-le-Bow (within the sound of whose bells you have to be born to be a true Cockney). The game ends with a child being caught between the joined arms of two others, emulating the act of chopping off their head! These sinister last lines were thought to have been added to the rhyme by children! During this time executions were common. I have thought twice about adding this game, with the words being so gruesome and not very politically correct. However, this was a game that I loved when I was small, so I have included it. It would be good if you could get your children to create more socially acceptable rhymes!

There are many old traditional songs that have lots of historical background. You can frequently check out the origins and meanings of these old rhymes by doing an internet search. I've included one of these websites in the Appendix.

Some ideas for in the classroom:

- Let the children choose an old singing and dancing rhyme, perhaps one of the above, and ask them to find out the history, meaning and significance of the words.

- Ask them to write new words using the same rhyme, which fit more with our culture today.

In the selection of ten singing and dancing games you will find many old familiar games, possibly from your childhood. Most of these games can be played indoors on a rainy day.

31. The Farmer's in His Den

Time: 10–15 minutes
Age Range: 4–11
Ideal Number of Players: 6+
Equipment Needed: None

How to Play

The players choose a 'farmer' and then form a circle around him holding hands.

They walk in a clockwise direction and chant, 'The farmer's in his den, the farmer's in his den. E, i, e, i, the farmer's in his den'.

This is then repeated with the words, 'The farmer wants a wife, the farmer wants a wife. E, i, e, i, the farmer wants a wife'.

The farmer chooses a wife from the circle of children. The wife joins him in the centre.

The chant continues with the following verses. After each verse, the previously elected child chooses someone from the circle to join the group in the middle.

Verse 3: The wife wants a child.

Verse 4: The child wants a nurse.

Verse 5: The nurse wants a dog.

Verse 6: The dog wants a bone.

The game ends with all players surrounding the child who has been chosen to be the bone. Together they all chant and pat the bone lightly, 'We all pat the bone, we all pat the bone. E, i, e, i, we all pat the bone'.

The bone then becomes the farmer and the game begins again.

Comments

When patting the bone, encourage players to be gentle. Remind players of the rule, 'We are kind and gentle, we don't hurt others'.

32. Pop Goes the Weasel

Time: 10–15 minutes
Age Range: 5–7
Ideal Number of Players: 6+
Equipment Needed: None

How to Play

The children join hands and form several circles of three or four players. Each circle has a weasel in the middle and there is one extra weasel outside.

Players dance and sing the following song:

> Half a pound of tuppenny rice,
> Half a pound of treacle.
> That's the way the money goes,
> Pop goes the weasel!

On the word 'pop', the weasels must run to a different circle and the extra weasel must try to get inside a circle before it is filled by another weasel.

There will always be one player who gets left out when the players change circles.

33. The Big Ship Sails on the Alley Alley O

Time: 10–25 minutes
Age Range: 4–7
Ideal Number of Players: 6+
Equipment Needed: None

How to Play

> The big ship sails on the alley alley O,
> The alley alley O, the alley alley O.
> The big ship sails on the alley alley O,
> On the last day of September.

At least five players stand in a line, holding hands.

Another player stands facing a wall, with her hands high against the wall to make an arch.

The head of the line leads everyone through the arch.

When the last player passes through the arch, the player making the arch turns around facing away from the wall with her arms crossed and held up.

The line now comes back around and they go through with the first person in the line making a new arch. When the last player passes through the arch, she turns and crosses her arms, holding hands with the previous arch.

The verse is repeated until all players have crossed arms and are holding hands with the first and last players joining to make a circle.

The rhyme then continues with:

> 'The captain said this will never, never do...' (players shake their heads gravely).

> 'The big ship sank to the bottom of the sea...' (players slowly squat and rise).

> 'We all dip our head in the deep blue sea...' (players bend their heads down as low as possible).

34. Ring a Ring o' Roses

Time: 10–15 minutes
Age Range: 5–7
Ideal Number of Players: 6+
Equipment Needed: None

How to Play

The players join hands and form a circle.

They skip in one direction as they sing the song below.

> Ring a ring o' roses,
> A pocket full of posies.
> Atishoo! Atishoo!
> We all fall down.
>
> Fishes in the water,
> Fishes in the sea.
> We all jump up,
> With a one, two, three.

At the end of verse one, the children sing, 'We all fall down', and the group usually falls down into a heap.

At the end of verse two, the children sing, 'We all jump up', and they all jump up with a one, two, three.

35. Sally Go Round the Sun

Time: 10–15 minutes
Age Range: 4–7 years
Ideal Number of Players: 6+
Equipment Needed: None

How to Play

> Sally go round the sun,
> Sally go round the moon.
> Sally go round the chimney pots,
> On a Sunday afternoon, whoo!

Players dance around in a circle facing inwards, reciting the rhyme.

When 'afternoon' is said, one player faces outwards.

The verse is repeated again with the children dancing in the opposite direction. When 'afternoon' is said, another player faces outwards and the game continues until all players are facing outwards.

36. Poor Jenny Stood a-Weeping

Time: 10–15 minutes
Age Range: 4–11
Ideal Number of Players: 6–20
Equipment Needed: None

How to Play

Poor Jenny Stood a-Weeping is a game that was played in the playgrounds of the 1950s and 1960s and was often initiated by children themselves. In this game, Jenny kneels with her hands to her face 'weeping' while the other children hold hands to form a circle and walk around her as they sing.

The child in the centre carries out the actions of the following verses and on the final verse 'stand up and choose your loved one', they stand up and choose a partner. The final verse has all the children skipping around.

Poor Jenny stood a-weeping, a-weeping, a-weeping,
Poor Jenny stood a-weeping, on a bright summer's day.

Why are you weeping, weeping, weeping?
Why are you weeping, on a bright summer's day?

I'm weeping for a loved one, a loved one, a loved one,
I'm weeping for a loved one, on a bright summer's day.

Stand up and choose your loved one, your loved one, your loved one,
Stand up and choose your loved one, on a bright summer's day.

And now she/he is so happy, so happy, so happy,
And now she/he is so happy, on a bright summer's day.

37. Oranges and Lemons

Time: 10 minutes
Age Range: 4–7
Ideal Number of Players: 12
Equipment Needed: None

How to Play

This is a game based around an old English children's song about the sounds of church bells in various parts of London.

Two children decide (in secret) who is 'oranges' and who is 'lemons' and then form an arch with both hands. The rest of the children dance (or run) through the arch while singing the rhyme. On 'Chip chop, chip chop' they lower the arch repeatedly, and on 'Chop off your head' they drop the arch to capture a child, who then has to choose oranges or lemons (again in secret, whispering) and stands behind the appropriate child. The game continues until everyone is caught and two lines are formed behind the original pair of children.

At the end of the game, there is usually a tug of war to test whether the oranges or lemons are stronger.

> Oranges and lemons, say the bells of St Clement's.
> You owe me five farthings, say the bells of St Martin's.
> When will you pay me? say the bells of Old Bailey.
> When I grow rich, say the bells of Shoreditch.
> When will that be? say the bells of Stepney.
> I'm sure I don't know, says the great bell at Bow.
>
> Here comes a candle to light you to bed,
> Here comes a chopper to chop off your head.
>
> Chip chop chip chop the last man's head.
> (The arch comes down tapping one player gently on the head.)

38. The Hokey Cokey

Time: 10 minutes
Age Range: 5–adult
Ideal Number of Players: 10+
Equipment Needed: None

How to Play

One person is chosen to be a group leader.

The players stand in a circle, holding hands.

The dance follows the instructions given in the lyrics of the song, which may be prompted by the leader.

> You put your right hand in, your right hand out,
> In, out, in, out, shake it all about.
> You do the hokey cokey and you turn around. That's what it's all about.

As the specific body parts are named, the players do the appropriate actions. At the end of each verse, the players sing the chorus.

> Woah the hokey cokey. Woah the hokey cokey.
> Woah the hokey cokey. Knees bent, arms stretch, ra, ra, ra.

For the chorus, all participants stand in the circle, holding hands. On each 'woah', they all raise their joined hands in the air and run in towards the centre of the circle, and on the 'hokey cokey', they all run backwards out again. On the last line they bend their knees then stretch their arms, as indicated, and for 'ra, ra, ra' they either clap in time or raise arms above their heads and push upwards in time to the music. More often than not, each subsequent verse and chorus is a little faster and louder. The next sequence begins with a new named body part and so it continues.

> left hand   right foot   left foot   whole self

Variations

If you have a large group playing this game and you find that it is becoming quite dangerous during the chorus, an alternative way of playing, which is much calmer and almost as much fun, is for the players to raise both their hands up above their head and wiggle their fingers when they are singing the chorus.

39. Heads, Shoulders, Knees and Toes

Time: 4–8 minutes
Age Range: 4–7
Ideal Number of Players: 6+
Equipment Needed: None

How to Play

The children sing the song:

> Heads shoulders, knees and toes,
> Knees and toes.
> Heads shoulders, knees and toes,
> Knees and toes.
> And eyes and ears and mouth and nose,
> Heads, shoulders, knees and toes.
> Knees and toes.

Actions

First time: touch each part of the body as it is mentioned.

Second time: keep action going but omit the word 'heads'.

Third time: keep pointing to each part as mentioned but omit saying 'heads' or 'shoulders'.

Fourth time: omit saying 'heads', 'shoulders' and 'knees', and so on until there are no words left, only actions.

40. Here We Go Round the Mulberry Bush

Time: 5 minutes
Age Range: 4–7
Ideal Number of Players: 8–12
Equipment Needed: None

How to Play

Chorus (to follow each verse)

> Here we go round the mulberry bush,
> The mulberry bush, the mulberry bush.
> Here we go round the mulberry bush,
> On a cold and frosty morning.

Verse 1

> This is the way we wash our hands,
> Wash our hands, wash our hands.
> This is the way we wash our hands,
> On a cold and frosty morning.

Verse 2

> This is the way we wash our face,
> Wash our face, wash our face.
> This is the way we wash our face,
> On a cold and frosty morning.

Verse 3

> This is the way we comb our hair,
> Comb our hair, comb our hair.
> This is the way we comb our hair,
> On a cold and frosty morning.

> This is the way we tie our shoes and so on.
> This is the way we go to school and so on.

> Chorus: All children skip round in a ring, holding hands.
> Verse: They stand still and perform the actions.

5 Skipping Games and Rhymes

Skipping Games and Rhymes

Skipping Games and Rhymes

Skipping games and rhymes have been featured in children's play for hundreds of years and in countries all over the world. Skipping is believed to have originated when rope-makers were forced to jump over strands of hemp as they twisted them together.

When I see children skipping in the playground, there is a never-ending stream of rhymes both new and old and children's faces are filled with smiles and laughter, while lunchtime supervisors merrily join in. Skipping is an activity that is inclusive of everyone, young, old, athletic and not so; it seems to bring joy to all involved and is of minimal financial cost to schools.

Sadly, during my years of running Positive Playtime training courses in schools, a frequent cry from teachers and lunchtime supervisors has been that children don't know how to play with a skipping rope or the traditional skipping rhymes and games we used to play.

With the advent of the internet, children hooked on online games and playing less outside with fears of stranger danger and busy roads, what was once a familiar sight in most homes and schools across the country seems to have diminished. In fact, I frequently see ropes in schools, wrapped around children's waists and used to play ponies, not what they were intended for!

I believe there is a role for us in re-igniting children's love of skipping and in teaching the traditional games and rhymes, which can then be passed down to the next generation and not be forgotten.

There are many possibilities for using a skipping rope other than just simply turning and jumping over a rope. Many students enjoy learning new tricks, which they love to show off to their friends.

There are skipping rhymes for groups, pairs and for those who want to skip solo.

Group Skipping Using a Long Rope

Games played by groups of children involve a long rope with one child turning it at each end. All children line up behind a rope turner and then each child has a turn. If they are singing a rhyme, all children sing the rhyme, while the individual child jumps or does the actions that the rhyme requires.

The simplest games are in-and-out games, with the children jumping through the rope in succession, first one jump, then two and so on. More complex games involve rhymes with actions, but the basic overall rule is the same: stop the rope and you're out and have to change places with either one of the rope turners or one of the children lining up to play.

You will find children love the long rope games and many of these can be taught in groups in the playground.

Skipping Rhymes with a Partner

This is for two players and they need a long enough rope so that they can both jump together.

Solo Skipping

A shorter rope is required and needs to be the right length, neither too long nor too short for the child to be able to jump over repetitively.

Skipping Rhymes

There are hundreds of rhymes with new ones or new variations being added all the time, but the old traditional ones still continue to be used and many of these are featured in this section. Some rhymes are obviously products of an older tradition, recited with little understanding but enthusiastic actions.

> I am a girl guide dressed in blue,
> These are the actions I must do:
> Salute to the King and bow to the Queen,
> And turn my back on the washing-machine.

Still surprisingly popular given the last king of England, George VI, died in 1952! The rhyme is recited to the rhythm of the skipping and actions performed for each line – salute, bow and turn around completely.

I encourage teachers to teach skipping skills and games once a term in their PE lessons.

Initially, I suggest they teach children how to skip solo; this gets them warmed up and learning some basic skills. The good thing about skipping is that it can be taught simultaneously to people with a range of abilities. It also allows different abilities to shine because of its non-competitive nature and children can strive for their personal best; so, everyone succeeds in their own way.

Once children have learnt the basic skills, they can then learn more complex moves that require greater agility and skill.

You will find that students enjoy learning new tricks which they love to show off to their friends.

Skipping Games and Rhymes

Like any equipment, it needs to be introduced and rules enforced as to how it's used; it also needs to be cared for and stored in a safe place.

Skipping Workshops

In some of the schools I have consulted with, they invite a trainer like myself or a professional skipper to run skipping workshops. They train a group of students, teaching them skills and tricks and then the whole school is invited to see a performance at the end of the day. Schools find these days very successful and often skipping fever hits their playgrounds and they are swarming with children skipping for months afterwards.

Benefits of Skipping

There are many benefits to children skipping, most notably the physical activity it offers. Sadly, childhood obesity levels are rising and the current statistics show that 20 per cent of Year 6 children are classified as obese (NHS England, 2020). Therefore, it is imperative schools encourage exercise and skipping is an ideal activity that suits all ability levels.

The British Heart Foundation's Jump Rope for Heart campaign is aimed at highlighting the health benefits of skipping. The events began over 35 years ago. You can sign up for free and receive £100 worth of skipping equipment to help your children get more active.

The British Skipping Association points out that it is an activity not only suited for recreation, but also a cardiovascular workout. This combination of an aerobic workout and co-ordination-building footwork has made rope skipping a popular form of exercise for many athletes.

Peter L. Lindsay and Denise Palmer's research (1981) further highlights that in many respects, traditional games are more beneficial to children's health (for example, their cardiovascular endurance) than formal syllabus games.

Benefits of Skipping

There are obviously many health and wellbeing benefits, and these are just a few:

- Improved cardiovascular fitness.

- Increased muscular strength

- Greater flexibility.

- Improved co-ordination

- Strong bones

- Children playing cooperatively in organised spaces

- Increased emotional wellbeing

- Opportunities for socialising, building social skills and developing friendships

- The promotion of children's learning, imagination, creative independence and interdependence

- Fun

- The development of confidence and self-esteem

- Stress reduction

Skipping can also improve your skills:

- Better timing and rhythm

- Improved balance

- Improved agility

Equipment

The equipment for skipping costs very little and can be made out of rope from a hardware store or plastic clothes lines. The beaded ropes or jump ropes are the best because they turn easily and are more easily controlled in tricks.

The British Heart Foundation's Jump Rope for Heart campaign will send free equipment and a teaching pack to a school for a sponsorship commitment (see the Appendix).

Photocopy this chapter and get a skipping craze going in your school today.

41. I Like Coffee, I Like Tea

Time: 10 minutes
Age Range: 5–11
Ideal Number of Players: 2
Equipment Needed: Two-person skipping rope

How to Play

This is a two-person skipping game.

The first player skips and sings:

> I like coffee, I like tea.
> I like (child's name), in with me.

The person named then joins in and they jump together with the new player singing.

> I hate coffee, I hate tea.
> I don't like (child's name), in with me.

In this instance, the first player is named and out.

The first player runs out and the rhyme starts again.

42. Cowboy Joe from Mexico

Time: 10 minutes
Age Range: 5–11
Ideal Number of Players: 6+
Equipment Needed: A long group skipping rope

How to Play

This is a group game.

Two players turn the rope.

All the other players line up by the side of one of the rope turners until it is their turn.

One player starts to skip and does the actions and they all sing:

> Cowboy Joe from Mexico,
> Hands up, stick 'em up,
> And out you go!

On 'out you go', the player stops jumping and runs to stand behind the rope turner. The game then starts again with a new player singing and doing the actions.

43. Snakes

Time: 10 minutes
Age Range: 6–11
Ideal Number of Players: 5+
Equipment Needed: One long skipping rope

How to Play

Two players hold the end of a long rope and wiggle the rope back and forth (at a suitable speed) so that it looks like a snake.

Everyone else is a jumper and they take turns trying to jump over the snake without touching it.

If a jumper touches the snake, he changes place with one of the players holding the end of the rope.

Variations

This game can also be played with the rope moving on the ground horizontally, where the jump must be a wide one rather than a high one.

44. Keep the Kettle Boiling

Time: 10 minutes
Age Range: 5–9
Ideal Number of Players: 6+
Equipment Needed: One long skipping rope

How to Play

Two players turn the rope.

All the other players are jumpers and line up by the side of one of the rope turners.

The rhyme for this goes:

> Keep the kettle boiling, never miss a beat.

Each person moves into the centre of the rope, jumps over the rope just once, while everyone sings the rhyme and then runs out as the next person runs in.

When they run out, they run around the back of the second rope turner, ready to come in again.

45. I'm a Little Bubble Car

Time: 6 minutes
Age Range: 5–11
Ideal Number of Players: 4+
Equipment Needed: One long skipping rope

How to Play

Two players turn the rope.

All the other players line up by the side of one of the rope turners until it is their turn.

The rhyme goes:

> I'm a little bubble car No. 48.
> I dash around the corner,
> And then put on my brakes.

At 'I dash around the corner', the skipper runs out and around the person turning the rope and then back into the middle.

At 'and then put on my brakes', the skipper stops the rope by straddling it ending with the rope between both legs.

The next skipper comes in and the game starts again.

46. Teddy Bear, Teddy Bear

Time: 10 minutes
Age Range: 6–11
Ideal Number of Players: 6+
Equipment Needed: One long skipping rope

How to Play

Two players turn the rope.

All the other players line up by the side of one of the rope turners until it is their turn.

One player starts to skip and does the actions while they all sing the rhyme:

> Teddy Bear, Teddy Bear turn around.
> Teddy Bear, Teddy Bear touch the ground.
> Teddy Bear, Teddy Bear climb the stairs.
> Teddy Bear, Teddy Bear say your prayers.
> Teddy Bear, Teddy Bear switch off the light.
> Teddy Bear, Teddy Bear say good night.

On 'good night', the child runs out.

The next skipper comes in once the player has finished the rhyme.

If a child becomes 'out' through not being able to jump the rope, missing their turn and so on, they become a rope turner.

Variations

You can use different words instead of 'Teddy Bear' such as 'Andy Pandy', 'butterfly', 'ladybird' and so on.

Comments

The skipper can add their own special touch to each move in this game.

47. Blue Bells, Cockle Shells

Time: 10 minutes
Age Range: 6–12
Ideal Number of Players: 6+
Equipment Needed: One long skipping rope

How to Play

Two players swing the rope back and forth. The third player is the jumper.

All other players line up by the side of one of the rope swingers until it is their turn.

> Everybody says the rhyme:
> Blue bells, cockle shells,
> Evey, ivey over.

The rope is rocked back and forth while the skipper jumps over it. At 'over', the rope is swung over his head and regular jumping begins. The rhyme continues:

> Mother's in the kitchen,
> Doing a bit of stitchin'.
> Father's in the workshop,
> Cutting up meat.
> Baby's in the cradle fast asleep.
> How many hours did the baby sleep?
> One, two, three... (and so on) OUT!

The skipper should skip more quickly on the numbers until 'out' is shouted. He should then move out to let the next skipper in.

48. All in Together Girls

Time: 10 minutes
Age Range: 5+
Ideal Number of Players: 6+
Equipment Needed: One very long skipping rope

How to Play

All in together, girls,
Never mind the weather girls,
When it is your birthday, please jump in.
January, February, March …

Continue through the calendar. Each skipper jumps in when her birthday month is called. Once all skippers are in the rope, the next rhyme is sung.

All in together, girls,
Never mind the weather girls,
When it is your birthday, please jump out.
January, February, March …

The skippers jump out when their birthday is called.

49. Helicopter

Time: 10 minutes
Age Range: 6–11
Ideal Number of Players: 6+
Equipment Needed: One long skipping rope

How to Play

All players except one are jumpers.

One player, called the Helicopter Pilot, stands in the middle of the jumpers. She holds one end of the rope and swings it around in a circle along the ground.

All jumpers jump over the rope as it comes by.

Anyone failing to clear the rope must take on the job of the pilot.

Comments

Change the pilot regularly to avoid dizziness.

It is important for the pilot to take care when swinging the rope since ankles can easily get hurt. It is good for the players to think about the rules that may be needed when playing this game.

50. Jelly on a Plate

Time: 10 minutes
Age Range: 6–11
Ideal Number of Players: 6+
Equipment Needed: One long skipping rope

How to Play

Two players turn the rope.

All other players line up by the side of one of the rope turners until it is their turn.

One player starts to skip and does the actions and they all sing the rhyme:

Jelly on a plate,
Jelly on a plate.
Wibble wobble,
Wibble wobble,
Jelly on a plate.

Sausages in the pan,
Sausages in the pan.
Sizzle bang,
Sizzle bang,
Sausages in the pan.

Baby on the floor,
Baby on the floor.
Pick it up,
Pick it up,
Baby on the floor.

Skippers should wiggle about when 'wibble wobble' is said.
Skippers should jump high when 'sizzle bang' is said.
Skippers should reach down to the floor when 'pick it up' is said.

The next skipper comes in once the rhyme has finished and it starts again.

6 Circle Games

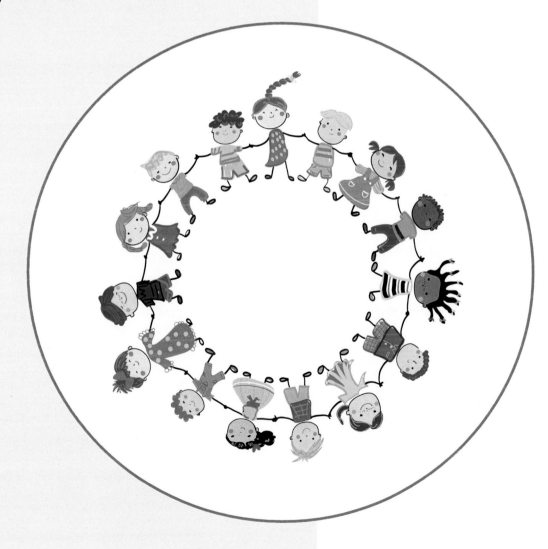

Circle Games

Circle Games

Groups of people and children have been sitting in circles since time began.

Circles are symbolic of unity, democracy and deep respect. In the wise traditions of old, indigenous people gathered in circles. Aboriginal and Maori tribes sat in circles and told stories; North American indigenous people passed the peace pipe.

Circle games by their nature are inclusive and co-operative, democratic and non-competitive. They can build self-esteem, co-operation, communication and positive relationships. When playing circle games, even the quietest of children can be encouraged to join in and nobody is ever left out. You will frequently see children in the playground gathering in circles and playing games.

I have chosen a selection of ten games for this section that can be played in the playground, at wet playtimes and in circle times too.

In the Playground

These games can be played standing or sitting. When the weather is good in the spring and summer months, these games work well on grassed areas. Old tarmac surfaces are often all that is required.

Wet Play

We sometimes struggle with thinking up games for wet playtimes. Please photocopy this section and keep it in your wet play box, ready for those rainy play days.

There is a whole playtime worth of activities here; all you need is a circle of chairs or carpet to sit on and the children will be happily entertained.

I hope that you will recognise many of these games. Simon Says is an old traditional game and easy to play with any age and anywhere. Honey I Love You and Granny's Green Undies are the games that produce the most laughter on my courses and which children repeatedly ask for!

Wishing you fun and laughter with this section!

51. Fruit Salad

Time: 10 minutes
Age Range: 4–11
Ideal Number of Players: 12+
Equipment Needed: Chairs if playing this at wet play

How to Play

Children sit in a circle; one person is nominated to be the leader and stands in the middle of the circle. She leaves an empty space on the ground, or if playing the game in the classroom, her chair is removed from the circle.

The leader stands in the centre of the circle and gives the first four children the name of four different fruits, for example apple, orange, lemon, banana. Then she continues giving the same four fruit names to the rest of the children around the circle.

The leader stands in the centre of the circle and calls out the name of one of the fruits, for example, apple.

All the apples stand up and move to another seat or space across the circle. They cannot sit in the seat next to them or in the same seat they were in before. The person standing also has to find a seat. Whoever is left without a seat becomes the new leader and the game starts again.

If 'fruit salad' is called, everyone must move.

The aim of the game is not to get left in the middle. If you are in the middle more than three times, then you are out of the game.

Variations

Instead of fruit, you can choose vegetables, trees, numbers or from a theme or topic you may be studying. Older children like the Simpson's theme – Bart, Homer, Lisa!

Comments

It is good to work out rules before playing this game and to sometimes reinforce throughout. An important rule is no running.

This game can be played on chairs at wet play and on grass, preferably, if playing outside.

52. Electric Current

Time: 15–25 minutes
Age Range: 5–adult
Ideal Number of Players: 10+
Equipment Needed: None

How to Play

Players sit in a circle either in the playground or on chairs in their classroom.

One player is chosen to be the 'electrician' and that person goes out of the room.

All the other players hold hands in such a way that the electrician, when standing inside the circle, will not be able to see their hands (usually hands are behind their backs).

One person is chosen to be the 'generator' and they start the current by gently squeezing the hand of the person next to them.

Several others are chosen to be various electrical appliances, for example, a telephone – ring, ring; a doorbell – ding, dong.

The electrician returns to the room and stands in the centre of the circle.

The generator starts the current going around the circle. Every time the current reaches an appliance, it must make an appropriate sound. When the current returns to the generator, it continues around the room again either clockwise or anti-clockwise.

The aim of the game is for the electrician to work out who the generator is.

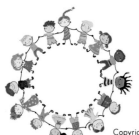

53. Apple Pie

Time: 10 minutes
Age Range: 5–9
Ideal Number of Players: 10+
Equipment Needed: None

How to Play

All players stand in a circle. One person is chosen to be a detective and they leave the circle.

One person is chosen to be 'it' and that person has to say 'apple pie' in a different voice from their own to disguise their identity from the detective.

The detective comes back and stands in the middle of the circle with their eyes closed.

They must try to guess who is saying 'apple pie'.

The detective has up to three guesses.

The person who is saying 'apple pie' is the next person to become the detective.

Variations

Once the game has been played a few times, move the players around.

54. Simon Says

Time: 10 minutes
Age Range: 4–11
Ideal Number of Players: 10+
Equipment Needed: None

How to Play

The players make a circle standing up.

One player is chosen to be 'Simon' and that person stands in the centre of the circle.

Simon then gives actions for the other players to follow. A few examples follow:

'Simon says touch your toes'.
'Simon says jump ten times on one foot'.
'Simon says wave your arms'.

Everyone must follow the instruction.

If Simon says, 'Touch your ears', and omits the words 'Simon says' before giving an instruction, the players must not do the action. If they do, then they are out of the game and have to sit down.

The last person who is standing can then be Simon!

Variations

You can vary the actions according to the age group of players you are playing with.

55. Zoom

Time: 10 minutes
Age Range: 5–11
Ideal Number of Players: 10+
Equipment Needed: None

How to Play

All players stand in a large circle and someone is chosen to lead the game.

Everyone is asked to imagine the word 'zoom' as the sound of a racing car.

The leader starts by saying 'zoom', and turning her head to the person on her left.

The next person passes the word 'zoom' to the next person and so on until everyone has quickly passed the word around the circle.

Next the leader explains that the word 'eek' makes the car stop and reverse direction.

Whenever the word 'eek' is said, the word 'zoom' goes in the opposite direction around the circle.

Keep it moving and don't let the sound slow down.

Variations

In a large group, you could have two sounds going round in different directions at the same time.

56. Conductor of the Orchestra

Time: 15 minutes
Age Range: 4–12
Ideal Number of Players: 10+
Equipment Needed: None

How to Play

The players form a circle.

One person is chosen to act as a detective. They may be blindfolded or leave the room or playground area.

One player is chosen to be the conductor of the orchestra.

The conductor stays in his place in the circle and starts an action such as clapping his hands together, stamping his feet, nodding his head, snapping fingers and so on. This is then copied by all the other players.

The detective returns and stands in the centre of the circle.

The aim of the game is for the detective to guess who the conductor of the orchestra is.

The detective has five guesses.

If he guesses correctly, then the conductor becomes the detective and a new conductor is chosen.

If the detective doesn't guess correctly, then a new detective and a new conductor are chosen.

Comments

Tell the conductor that they need to change the action regularly (every 10–15 seconds).

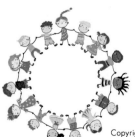

57. Granny's Green Undies

Time: 10 minutes
Age Range: 5–12
Ideal Number of Players: 10+
Equipment Needed: None

How to Play

Everyone stands in a circle.

One person is chosen to stand in the middle and be Granny.

The aim of the game is for the players to try to get Granny out by each asking funny questions to which she always has to reply, 'Granny's green undies' and keep a straight face (which is often hard).

Players in the circle take turns at asking questions like, 'What do you brush your teeth with?'

If Granny laughs, she must change places with the person who asked the question and the game starts again.

Comments

Try to think up different and interesting questions. They will produce lots of laughter!

58. Statues

Time: 6 minutes
Age Range: 6–11
Ideal Number of Players: 10+
Equipment Needed: None

How to Play

All the players stand in a circle.

One person is 'on' and goes into the centre. They give instructions to the others such as hop, scratch your head, pull a face.

At some point they call 'stop' and all the players in the circle must freeze in that position.

The person who is 'on' tries to make people laugh (by pulling faces, making jokes).

Anyone who does laugh becomes 'on' and replaces the person in the centre.

Comments

This game is almost the reverse of Granny's Green Undies!

59. Who Stole the Cookies from the Cookie Jar?

Time: 10 minutes
Age Range: 4+
Ideal Number of Players: 10+
Equipment Needed: None

How to Play

Players stand or sit in a circle and are all numbered 1–10+.

A leader is chosen.

Each player starts to alternatively pat their own knees and clap their hands. This action – pat, clap, pat, clap, pat, clap – continues as the chant is sung.

Players chant, 'Who stole the cookies from the cookie jar?'

The leader chants, 'Number (for example, five) stole the cookies from the cookie jar'.

Number five then responds, 'Who, me?'

Everyone replies, 'Yes, you!'

Number five chants, 'Couldn't be!'

Everyone replies, 'Then who?'

Number five replies, 'Number (for example, 12) stole the cookies from the cookie jar!'

Number 12 then continues with, 'Who me?' and the chant continues as before.

The idea of the game is to keep the rhythm of pats and claps going while continuing the chant with a new number being called each time. As the children get used to the game, the leader can speed it up.

Variations

For very young children, instead of having numbers, the children's names are used. The leader places a cookie jar in front of her. She starts the game by looking in the empty

cookie jar and saying, 'Who stole the cookies from the cookie jar?' Then she points to a child and says their name, for example, 'Adele stole the cookies from the cookie jar'. The game continues until all the children have had a turn. A fun ending is for the leader to confess, 'All right, I confess. I stole the cookies from the cookie jar and here they are'. The leader passes around a plate of cookies for each child to take one.

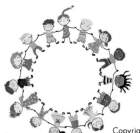

60. Honey I Love You

Time: 10 minutes
Age Range: 4–12
Ideal Number of Players: 8+
Equipment Needed: None

How to Play

All the players stand or sit in a circle.

One player is chosen to be 'it' and stand in the middle. This player must approach another player in the circle and ask: 'Honey I love you; won't you give me a smile?'

The person being questioned must answer, 'Honey, I love you, but I just can't smile'.

If this person does smile or laugh, he becomes 'it' and stands in the middle and the previous 'it' joins the circle of students.

The person who is 'it' is not allowed to touch other players but may make as many gestures and funny faces as he wishes.

Comments

Very few rules restrict how the victim is provoked into smiling. Sometimes the 'no touching' rule does not take effect, but it depends on whether you want to play it this way or not.

7 Parachute Games

Parachute Games

The parachute was originally used in the late 18th century to support people in falling safely from the sky. Polish aviator Jodaki Kuparaento was the first to use a parachute as an emergency lifesaving device on 24 July 1808, when he jumped from a balloon that was on fire. Since this first jump to safety, parachutes have saved thousands of lives. In the 1960s, many parachutes could be found in army and navy surplus stores, and it was during this time that 'many playful pioneers' found the opportunity and inspiration to create new recreational and physical education activities (Le Fevre, 2006).

In the late 1990s, I was lucky enough to be given an ex-Air-Force wartime parachute by Mildred Masheder, well known for her books and work on co-operative group games. It was my first parachute and is made of strong silk. The children and adults I have worked with over the years have had great fun playing with it.

Today there are many educational suppliers who produce parachutes specifically to play games on the ground.

Parachute games are extremely popular and can be used with any age, from nursery children to teenagers and with adults in team-building events! The games are great fun, encourage physical fitness, co-operation, non-competitive play and reinforce turn-taking, sharing and teamwork. When playing with a parachute, everyone shares the same piece of equipment at the same time, unlike games such as football, rugby, netball and hockey.

The games and activities in this section contain some new activities and many of the old favourites which teachers, lunchtime supervisors and youth leaders love.

I have included some physically active and some quieter, gentler games. When starting the games, care and consideration needs to be taken in explaining some basic rules to the children so that you and they get the maximum fun out of the activities.

Rules and Safety

The nature of parachute games means that children are generally very active; this means that we need to make sure that children are safe and don't get hurt. If you begin each session explaining some basic rules, then the risk of injury will be reduced.

- Ask the children to remove their shoes before playing with the parachute.

- Encourage the children to space themselves around the parachute evenly so that there are no large gaps.

- Ensure the children hold the parachute securely with both hands, with their thumb and fingers on top.

- The children should take care of those either side of them as elbows can cause injury.

- The children are to be respectful of the parachute and not to pull too hard or kick it.

- Always inform the children that you will only select them as the game leader if they are sitting down quietly and not shouting out.

- If the parachute has a hole in the middle, then please ensure that the children know it is dangerous to place their head through the centre.

Ages

Parachute games are for all age children and adults. However, you will need to evaluate each game against the age of the children, taking into consideration the level of risk and the complexity of instructions needed for some games.

Numbers

The larger the parachute, the more children can participate, for example, a five-metre parachute will be large enough for about 20 children. A seven-metre parachute is ideal for the average class.

61. Mushroom

Time: 5–10 minutes
Age Range: 5+
Ideal Number of Players: 10+
Equipment Needed: Parachute

How to Play

The children squat down and hold the parachute taut on the ground.

When someone shouts, 'One, two, three, mushroom', the children all rise up to full height with arms above their heads to inflate the parachute. A giant mushroom is formed.

Have the players stand still and watch as the parachute settles slowly to the ground.

Players take it in turn to call out, 'One, two, three, mushroom'.

Variations

Instead of 'one, two, three, mushroom', the player could call out the name of any fruit or vegetable, for example, 'carrots, potatoes, broccoli, mushroom'.

Floating Mushroom – the same as Mushroom except on 'mushroom', everyone releases the parachute at the same time (ideally!) and the parachute floats up to the sky!

Comments

This game involves teamwork, is not hard and looks stunning – a great photo opportunity!

62. The Mongolian Tent and Whisper Game

Time: 10 minutes
Age Range: 5+
Ideal Number of Players: 12+
Equipment Needed: Parachute

How to Play

The children play Mushroom as in Game 61.

The Mongolian Tent

All the players sit inside the parachute after the giant, billowing mushroom effect has occurred and keep in position by sitting on the edge of the parachute and leaning against the 'walls'.

The Whisper Game

The children remain seated while one person is named the leader. This person secretly whispers a sentence to the person next to her and this sentence continues around the circle until it reaches the last person, who then recites out loud the sentence he has heard.

The leader verifies if the sentence is accurate or not – generally there are inaccuracies and sometimes players purposely change the sentence along the way!

The game continues with a new leader.

63. Row, Row, Row Your Boat

Time: 5 minutes
Age Range: 4–7
Ideal Number of Players: 8+
Equipment Needed: Parachute

How to Play

The players sit around the parachute with their feet and legs under the parachute.

They take hold of the parachute's edges with both hands and rock back and forth, as if they are rowing, while singing:

Row, row, row your boat,
Gently down the stream.
Merrily, merrily, merrily, merrily,
Life is but a dream.

Row, row, row your boat,
Gently down the stream.
If you see a crocodile,
Don't forget to scream.
Argh!

Variations

Once the song is finished, you can suggest that the players lie very still and finish off with a game of Sleeping Lions. In this game, the players lie as still as they can under the parachute. If you see them move, you touch them gently and they then very quietly and slowly stand up and move out of the circle.

64. Blow the Ball

Time: 10 minutes
Age Range: 5+
Ideal Number of Players: 12+
Equipment Needed: Parachute, two table tennis balls

How to Play

The players hold the parachute and lift it up to their chins.

One or more table tennis balls are placed in the parachute.

Blow the ball or balls around the parachute one player at a time.

Variations

Play tag with two different coloured table tennis balls. Hit each other's balls by blowing them against one another.

Blow using two different coloured table tennis balls. Which ball gets around the parachute first?

65. Making Waves

Time: 6 minutes
Age Range: 7+
Ideal Number of Players: 12+
Equipment Needed: Large ball, parachute

How to Play

All the players stand in a circle holding the parachute.

A large ball is given to one of the players, who then places it in the parachute.

The ball then moves from player to player, while they make waves with the parachute.

You can get the game to go faster by, for example, shouting the children's names.

Comments

The parachute's waves and colours make this an amazing sight.

66. Team Ball

Time: 10–15 minutes
Age Range: 6+
Ideal Number of Players: 10+
Equipment Needed: Coloured balls, parachute with a hole in the centre

How to Play

Divide the group into two teams.

Each team has its own coloured balls.

The balls need to be able to go through the hole in the middle of the parachute to score a goal.

Choose a ball boy or girl from each team. Their role is to catch balls that fall out of the parachute and put them back in. This speeds the game up.

Place both balls on the parachute.

The players now make the parachute mushroom (small movements up and down).

Teams score one point for every ball that goes through the hole.

The team that gets the most points wins.

67. Rockabye

Time: 10–15 minutes
Age Range: 4+
Ideal Number of Players: 12+
Equipment Needed: Parachute

How to Play

The parachute is folded in half or rolled up.

A player is then chosen to lie in the parachute.

The rest of the players hold the edges of the parachute and rock the child to and fro as if he were in a hammock.

Variations

The parachute is fully laid out on the ground. A small number of players lie in a circle with their feet to the middle. They can be lifted gently off the ground and slowly revolved around.

Alternatively, lay the parachute on the ground. One player is chosen to sit or lie in the middle. She is then lifted up, cradled and rocked backwards and forwards.

Comments

There are many ways of rocking young people in a parachute and indeed adults often enjoy being rocked too, if there are strong enough volunteers!

68. Spinning

Time: 10 minutes
Age Range: 4+
Ideal Number of Players: 12+
Equipment Needed: Parachute

How to Play

Young people adore this game and it produces lots of excitement and merriment. I have found that secondary school children and even adults love it too!

The parachute is laid down on the ground.

One player sits in the centre. The other players stand holding onto the edge of the parachute.

These players then start moving in a clockwise direction while the person in the centre of the parachute remains firmly seated.

Players can sing:

> Here we go round the mulberry bush,
> The mulberry bush, the mulberry bush.
> Here we go round the mulberry bush,
> On cold and frosty mornings.

As the players move around the seated player, they start to wrap the seated player in the parachute in a cocoon-like way.

Once the seated player is wrapped up to her shoulders, the group pulls the parachute outwards, thus spinning the child in the middle on her bottom.

Comments

Caution: When wrapping the child in the parachute, please only go as far as the shoulders. Identify to the group the dangers of wrapping the parachute around the neck of the player.

69. Group Balance

Time: 5 minutes
Age Range: 7+
Ideal Number of Players: 10+
Equipment Needed: Parachute

How to Play

The players roll the edge of the parachute inwards several times and tuck their fingers in under the roll so that they have a strong grip.

They then stand up.

One person tells everyone to lean back at exactly the same time. It helps to say, 'We will lean back on three. One, two, three'.

The parachute will get tighter and tighter.

If all players work together, they should be able to lean back quite far without losing their balance.

Variations

For an added challenge, ask players to turn their backs to the parachute, reach behind themselves for a grip, and then try and balance outward.

Comments

Make sure you have a strong parachute for this exercise.

Play the game on a soft surface such as grass.

70. Crossover

Time: 10–15 minutes
Age Range: 6+
Ideal Number of Players: 10+
Equipment Needed: Parachute

How to Play

When the parachute is inflated to a count of 'One, two, three, mushroom!', the facilitator can call out instructions to cross beneath the parachute while it is still billowing, for example, 'All those who are wearing green' or 'Those who had toast for breakfast'.

The facilitator can also call out players' names and those players cross under the parachute.

Sometimes everyone crosses, for example, 'All those who like school holidays', and then the parachute has to be caught before it finally sinks to the ground.

8 Quiet Games

Quiet Games

Quiet Games

Are any of these scenarios familiar? Are there children in your school who:

- don't enjoy running around at playtimes?

- would rather sit in quiet contemplation, maybe in a quiet area of the playground, a garden or more solitary space?

- would prefer to read a book or play a quiet game or activity?

If you have answered yes to any of the above, then it's time to create a quiet space and offer the choice of quieter games and activities.

During my many years as an educational consultant, adviser, teacher and parent, I have listened to worried parents' concerns over their child going out to play and children who seem averse to playing in the playground. Some years ago, I had a parent approach me in the summer months who explained that her son dreaded summer because he was expected to play cricket and do sports at lunchtime, which he hated. He felt like other children wouldn't want to be his friend and ultimately that he just didn't fit in.

This child was in my gifted and talented class, and all he wanted to do was play quietly, read, create or play music. He was a hugely talented child with enormous potential and needed a space to feel like he did 'fit in'.

Educationally, it is important that we offer children a breadth of experience, and playtime is no exception. We can provide children with a range of games and activity zones which cater for all our children's varying needs. Here are some ideas:

- Teach all children the quiet games from this section in their PE lessons.

- Ensure that quiet games are played regularly.

- Create a quiet zoned activity area with picnic tables, rugs and mats when the weather permits.

- Organise quiet games activity boxes for the quiet zoned area. These may include books, board games, Lego, cards, colouring, jigsaws, bricks, farm animals and so on.

- Create a secret garden or quiet space away from the busy playground. If you have access to a green area or garden, then this is perfect.

- Develop a gardening club. Many children like to connect with nature at playtime.

71. The Weather Game

Time: 10 minutes
Age Range: 4–9
Ideal Number of Players: 10+
Equipment Needed: None

How to Play

All players sit in a circle.

The leader wriggles her ten fingers and explains that she is making rain.

She then passes the rain on to the person next to her and they likewise pass the rain to the person next to them and so forth, until everyone in the circle has raining fingers.

Once the rain has come back to the leader, she changes the action to sunshine, where she folds her arms and smiles at the player sitting next to her and the beautiful smiles are passed around the circle.

When the sunshine reaches the leader, she tells the players that they are all going to make big sunshine rays with their arms and they then stretch up their arms and hands to mime sunshine rays and then they put their hands gently in their lap and the game is finished.

Variations

If you are looking for a livelier, noisier game, then after passing the rain the players can pass the thunder, patting their knees loudly to make the thunder sound!

Alternatively, if you are looking for a short, uplifting game, you can get the players to pass a smile around the circle.

Comments

This is a good wet weather game.

72. Sleeping Angels

Time: 10 minutes
Age Range: 6–12
Ideal Number of Players: 10–30
Equipment Needed: Blindfold for the detective

How to Play

All the children sit in a circle.

One person is chosen to be a detective; the remaining children are the angels.

If this game is being played in a classroom, the detective is normally asked to leave the room. If they are playing outside, the detective normally wears a blindfold.

While the detective is out of the room or blindfolded, a person is secretly chosen to be the sleepmaker.

The detective is then called back to the centre of the circle.

The sleepmaker then proceeds to try to put the angels to sleep by winking at them without the detective seeing.

Any players winked at must 'fall asleep' immediately.

The detective's job is to guess who the sleepmaker is before all the angels fall asleep. The detective has three guesses.

Variations

This game is often referred to as Wink Murder and can be played in a similar way with the sleepmaker being substituted for a murderer. When players are winked at and thus murdered, they make lots of noise, writhe on the floor, make last requests and so on. A lot more dramatic and a noisier game!

73. Donkey

Time: 10–15 minutes
Age Range: 7–12
Ideal Number of Players: 6+
Equipment Needed: A ball

How to Play

The players stand in a circle.

They pass the ball from one player to another.

The ball can be thrown to any player and doesn't have to go in any particular direction.

The players need to stay alert and concentrate. If they miss catching the ball, they gain a letter of the word 'donkey', for example, 'd'.

Once a player has collected all the letters of the word 'donkey', they are out and have to sit down.

The last player left is the winner.

74. Pass the Keys

Time: 10–15 minutes
Age Range: 6–11
Ideal Number of Players: 10+
Equipment Needed: Chairs (optional), keys

How to Play

The players sit in a very tight circle with no gaps or spaces.

Everyone sitting in the circle has their hands behind their back.

One person is chosen to stand in the middle with their eyes closed.

A player is chosen to go around the outside of the circle and give a set of keys to one of the players.

The person in the centre then uncovers her eyes.

The children who are seated try to pass the set of keys around the circle without the person in the middle seeing or hearing.

The person in the middle has to try to guess who has the keys. They are allowed three guesses.

When the person in the centre correctly guesses, a new middle person is chosen and the game starts again.

75. The Whisper Game

Time: 10 minutes
Age Range: 7–11
Ideal Number of Players: 6+
Equipment Needed: None

How to Play

The players remain seated in a circle while one person is named the leader.

The leader secretly whispers a sentence such as 'My dog's name is Oscar' to the person next to her and this sentence continues around the circle until it reaches the last person, who then recites out the sentence he has heard.

The leader verifies if the sentence is accurate or not. Generally, there are inaccuracies and sometimes players purposely change the sentence along the way!

The game continues with a new leader.

Variations

This game can also be played with a parachute (see Game 62).

Comments

In The Whisper Game, cumulative errors from mishearing often result in the sentence heard by the last player differing greatly and amusingly from the one uttered by the first. This game is often invoked as a metaphor for cumulative error, especially the inaccuracies of rumours or gossip.

76. Addabout

Time: 10 minutes
Age Range: 7–11
Ideal Number of Players: 10+
Equipment Needed: None

How to Play

All the players stand in a circle.

The leader makes one simple movement, for example, a spiral movement with their finger.

The next person makes a spiral movement plus another movement, for example, a foot stamp.

This continues around the circle with each person adding a movement.

No talking. If someone misses or talks, then they are out.

77. How Do You Do?

Time: 10 minutes
Age Range: 4–6
Ideal Number of Players: 6+
Equipment Needed: None

How to Play

This fun game includes a little rhyme.

Everyone sits or stands in a circle.

A player turns to the person next to them, shakes their hand and says, 'Hello (name of person). How do you do? Who's that sitting next to you?'

This player looks at the person next to them, shakes their hand and says, 'It's (name of person). Hello. How do you do? Who's that sitting next to you?'

The game continues until everyone in the circle has had a go.

Comments

This is a great game to play at the start of term when you've new classes and children. It's a good, fun way for children to learn each other's names in an informal way.

78. The Writing Game

Time: 10 minutes
Age Range: 4–11
Ideal Number of Players: 8+
Equipment Needed: None

How to Play

Ask the players to get into pairs and choose who is to be A and who is B.

Ask A to close her eyes while B 'writes' on his partner's palm. He can write a word, letter or draw a shape with one finger. Encourage the players to decide whether to use upper and lower case letters and determine any punctuation which may be needed.

Encourage clear and exact writing.

The player who is receiving the message tries to guess what it is and may ask for a repeat if necessary.

Comments

Start with simple words and shapes.

79. There's a Space on My Right

Time: 10 minutes
Age Range: 6–11
Ideal Number of Players: 12+
Equipment Needed: Circle of chairs

How to Play

Players sit in a circle with an empty chair.

The person to the left of the empty chair says, 'There's a space on my right and I'd like (person's name) to come and sit in it'.

The named person then crosses the circle and sits in the chair.

This then leaves another empty chair on someone else's right! The game then continues as above.

Comments

This can be a good getting-to-know-you game. It is also a good wet play game.

80. I Went Shopping

Time: 10 minutes
Age Range: 8+
Ideal Number of Players: 15+
Equipment Needed: None

How to Play

All players sit in a circle.

The first person starts with, 'I went shopping and bought a/some (name of something, for example, apples)'.

The next person repeats, 'I went shopping and bought some apples and some (name of their item)'.

This continues around the circle with everyone repeating the shopping that has been bought and adding something else.

Variations

There is a movement version of this where the first player makes a movement (for example, clapping hands), the second player then repeats and adds another move and so on.

Comments

Nobody needs be out if they forget anything. The person who thought of it can remind them of it.

9 Co-Operative Games

Co-Operative Games

Co-Operative Games

You can learn more about an individual during an hour of play than in a year of conversation.

Plato

Many adults and even young people don't play games anymore because of negative experiences they had with physical education classes in school and with competitive sports. They felt left out, not good enough, like losers. Yet play, and friendship are therapeutic for everyone.

Maheshvarananda (2017)

One of the reasons I love co-operative games is that nobody is ever 'out', there are no winners, no losers, no outsiders; it is purely a win-win situation.

Many of the games I have included in this book are co-operative by nature. This section is wholly dedicated to co-operative games, which are to be played just for the fun of it.

As Masheder (1997) says,

> In co-operative games all players find it mutually beneficial to help one another. It is a case of working together, making joint decisions, and doing your best. So, the challenge comes from the process rather than being a winner.

There is of course a place for competitive games, and everyone likes to win at games. In the last two decades, non-competitive games have grown in popularity. Thankfully, it looks like a balance between competitive and non-competitive games is now emerging.

All play has a great element of co-operation. In practice, there must be mutual agreement on rules, and in team games and sport there is a tremendous group spirit which produces strong cohesion and mutual respect.

> It is interesting to know that in many early societies there are well-established traditions of co-operative games that were played by adults and children alike. Human beings are by their very nature co-operative, although in our troubled modern world this doesn't always appear to be the case. In fact, we could never have survived as human beings if we had not helped each other throughout our long evolution. In many cultures the very notion of competing against each other was a completely alien concept. In certain societies this still exists, although outside influences have been gradually eroding it. What still remains are the many cooperative leisure activities that have

always been an intrinsic part of the culture, and these include not only games but communal dance, drama and song.

Masheder (1997)

In researching this section, I discovered a whole wealth of benefits to co-operative games. I hope that these games help foster a spirit of co-operation in your school and classroom.

Co-operative games foster:

- kindness and sharing

- empathy

- collaboration

- peace and harmony

- enhanced self-concept

- positive communication skills

- peaceful conflict-solving

- feelings of goodwill towards others

- mutual decision-making

- inclusion

- reduced anxiety in having to win and otherwise appear a failure

- affirmation and encouragement by others

- enjoyment

- fun

Cooperative games are revolutionary in the potential to create a better world. If we want to build strong people with moral values and a love for humanity, we can take a step in that direction, with laughter and charm, by playing these games.

Maheshvarananda (2017)

81. Heads Down, Thumbs Up

Time: 10 minutes
Age Range: 6–11
Ideal Number of Players: 12–30
Equipment Needed: None

How to Play

Choose two or more children to stand up.

All the others put their heads down with their eyes closed and thumbs sticking up.

The two left standing must then creep around and gently touch one person each on the thumb.

Everyone is then told to open their eyes and the children who were touched stand up and try to guess which child touched them.

The goal is for the players to correctly guess the person who touched his or her thumb.

If they get it right, the children swap places; if not the children have another go.

Comments

This is a good quiet game as well as a co-operative one.

82. The Bean Game

Time: 10 minutes
Age Range: 5–adult
Ideal Number of Players: 8–30
Equipment Needed: None

How to Play

One person is chosen to be the leader.

The leader explains the different categories of beans and demonstrates the actions for each.

French bean – the players say, 'Bonjour', and bow down.

Jelly bean – the players wobble like jelly.

Baked bean – the players lie down on the floor in a stretched-out position.

Broad bean – the players make a standing starfish shape.

Kidney bean – the players lie curled up on the floor.

Chilli bean – the players shiver.

Frozen bean – the players freeze (stay still).

The leader calls a bean and all the players have to do the actions of that bean.

Variations

Since this is a co-operative game, children do not get 'out'. However, an adaptation of this, which would make the game more competitive, would be for the last child doing the bean action to be out, the winner being the last person left in.

I prefer the co-operative version!

Comments

This is a great energising game and is also good for wet play days. It is extremely popular with older children and adults love it too!

83. Huggy Bear

Time: 10–15 minutes
Age Range: 6+
Ideal Number of Players: 15–30
Equipment Needed: Access to music

How to Play

A group leader is selected. They operate the music and call the numbers.

Players stand around randomly in the room or selected playground space.

When the music starts, they all move around in any direction.

As the music stops, a number is called out by the leader and the players quickly 'Huggy Bear', that is, they join together by hugging other members of the group with the selected number of players. For example, if number eight is called, the players have to get into a group of eight and 'Huggy Bear'.

Those children who cannot make up a group of that number get together while the music re-starts to choose the next number to be called.

Variations

This game can also be played without hugging, with players just gathering in a group of the said number.

This simple method can be applied to other possibilities: height, anyone wearing the colour green, blue eyes and so on.

Comments

This is a very useful way of getting young people into groups quickly without any stress ('will I be chosen?').

84. All Change

 Time: 10–25 minutes
Age Range: 6–10
Ideal Number of Players: 10–25
Equipment Needed: None

How to Play

Players form a large circle with everybody on their hands and knees.

All players are numbered one or two.

When number ones are called, they must all move one 'pace' forward.

When number twos are called, they do likewise.

The aim of the game is for all players to attempt to cross the circle to the other side. However, in the centre, a great deal of co-operation will be needed to navigate successfully.

85. Points of Contact

Time: 10 minutes
Age Range: 6–12
Ideal Number of Players: 10–25
Equipment Needed: None

How to Play

Explain to the group that there are nine points of the body that can touch the floor in this game – two feet, two hands, two elbows, two knees and one forehead.

Ask the players to work by themselves initially.

The idea is that you call a number from one to nine and each player must touch the floor with that number of points.

Once players are confident working individually, ask them to work in pairs, then groups of three, four and so on.

Variations

Progress to a number that means that some of the group will have to be carried or lifted by others!

Comments

This game encourages group co-operation.

86. Noisy Animals

Time: 10–15 minutes
Age Range: 4–11
Ideal Number of Players: 5+
Equipment Needed: None

How to Play

Assign each child to an animal but don't let the rest of the group know who is which animal.

Make sure that there are at least two of each type of animal.

The objective of the game is for each child to find another person who is the same animal, so in the end, the pairs or groups of animals are together.

The players have to go around making the sound of their animals and moving like their animals.

Possible animals include dog, cat, mouse, lion, wolf, elephant, cow and so on.

Variations

Instead of using sound, older players can use their detective skills by asking the different players a variety of questions to tease out what kind of animal they are. Closed questions need to be used which have to be answered with a yes or no response. For instance, 'Do you live on a farm?' or 'Do you live in the jungle?' or 'Are you an animal that I would stroke?'

87. Co-Operative Letters

Time: 5–10 minutes
Age Range: 6–9
Ideal Number of Players: 10+
Equipment Needed: None

How to Play

This game can be played indoors or outside on a grassed area if available.

Suggest that the players work in groups of two or three.

Ask them to make various letters of the alphabet using their bodies to form the letter shapes. Players can do this standing, lying down, kneeling, sitting, curling into the appropriate shape and so on.

Suggest that they try and build words using the whole group – how about co-operation?

Comments

This is a good wet weather game.

88. The Laughing Circle

Time: 10 minutes
Age Range: 5–11
Ideal Number of Players: 10–20
Equipment Needed: None

How to Play

The first person lies down on his back. The second lies down on his back with his head on the first one's stomach. The third lies with her head on the second one's stomach and so on.

The first one says 'ha' while trying not to laugh, the second follows with 'ha, ha' and so on.

This game generally ends up with the players in roars of laughter.

You can try other sounds in the same way, for example, 'ho' or 'hee'.

Variations

If the players are averse to lying on one another, you can organise the players to lie down, face upwards in a circle with their heads placed close together and their bodies lying down as if they are all spokes in a wheel. As above, they can use the same sounds, and you get just as much laughter.

89. Tangles

Time: 10 minutes
Age Range: 6–11
Ideal Number of Players: 7–12
Equipment Needed: None

How to Play

The players form a small, tight circle.

They all hold out their left hand and they take hold of the left hand of someone else in the group but not the person beside them.

They then hold out their right hand and take hold of the right hand of a different person – not their neighbour and not the person whose left hand they are holding.

The players then have to try and untangle themselves without letting go of their hands by going over, around and under each other.

Comments

It often helps if you have one or two children directing things from the sidelines and helping to stop players from falling over.

This is a great co-operative activity that is also quiet. A whole-class tangle, this could take a long time to untangle!

90. Follow the Leader

Time: 10–15 minutes
Age Range: 4–11
Ideal Number of Players: As many as want to play
Equipment Needed: None

How to Play

One player is chosen to be the leader.

The players form a single line behind the leader, one behind the other, all facing in the same direction.

The players follow the leader's speed, directions, arm movements and so on.

Walking:

- forward, backwards, sideways

- along a line, in circles, in curves

- in a zig-zag

- low and tall

- on heels or toes

- fast, slow

- big steps, small steps, wide steps, narrow steps

- knees lifted high in front

- legs kicked out straight in front (like a wooden soldier)

- on the spot

Arm movements:

- pushing arms out above your head, at chest height, to your sides

- circling arms forwards across your body and backwards

- single arm punches upwards, forwards and sideways

- arms extended overhead and out to the side

Variations

Jogging instead of walking.

Players follow the leader but walk together as a group rather than in a line.

Comments

Follow the leader can be played either as a quiet game, or as a noisier, more active game. The choice is yours!

10 Games from Around the World

91. Four Square (New Zealand)
92. Caught You (China)
93. Clap Ball (Cameroon)
94. Korepe (Turkey)
95. Ambulance (Sweden)
96. Catch the Chicks (Taiwan)
97. Sardines (Germany)
98. Daaba Doobi (Pakistan)
99. Countries (Romania)
100. Dakpanay (Philippines)
101. Match My Feet (Democratic Republic of Congo)

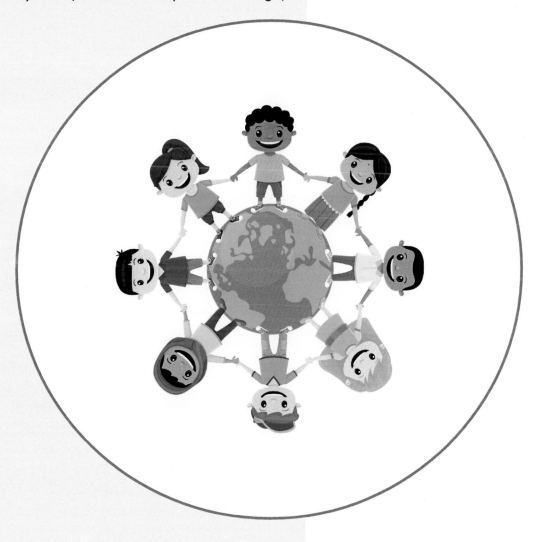

Games from Around the World

Games from Around the World

Children from all over the world have one thing in common: they love to play games.

The games in this book are intended as a tool through which students can learn about other cultures in a creative and fun way. Discover in this section how children from New Zealand, China, Cameroon, Turkey, Sweden, Taiwan, Germany, Pakistan, Romania, the Philippines and the Democratic Republic of Congo play traditional games.

When working in London, I used to hear a lot about the game Four Square from the children. This game was often brought over by Kiwi teachers. In 2002 we moved to New Zealand and lived there until 2009, so I was lucky enough to be taught how to play the game by a group of children at my daughter's school. Four Square is a firm favourite over there and frequently played at playtimes. The teachers also used to tell me that the game gets the children active and using their imagination.

Ideas for using this section:

* Find a world map and mark in the above countries.

* Before playing each game, look up where the country is located on the map and talk about the country and its culture.

* Think about how play may be influenced by the climate.

* Make flags and stick them on the world map.

* Use the additional template in the resources section at the back of the book to add your own games from other countries. You may like to email me these games.

Many cultures enjoy games that typically are non-competitive. The emphasis is on communal spirit, shared fun and healthy exercise. Satisfaction comes through playing, not winning. Other cultures incorporate a more competitive spirit into their games. By the end of an exciting activity, a specific team or individual enjoys recognition as the winner.

Games from other countries should be viewed with respect and appreciation.

You will find that some of these games are very similar to games you already know and love. Ambulance from Sweden is very similar to Hospital Tag, and Sardines from Germany is in fact a popular game universally.

I hope that through these activities, your children will have the opportunity to achieve a deeper understanding and appreciation of other cultures.

Games from Around the World

91. Four Square (New Zealand)

Time: 20 minutes
Age Range: 7–11
Ideal Number of Players: 8+
Equipment Needed: One large ball

How to Play

1	2
3	4

The four square should be approximately three metres square.

One player occupies each square, and the other players wait behind a line for a turn. Number four player serves by bouncing the ball in his own square then hitting it into any other square. The player who receives the ball tries to hit it into any other square. The rally continues until a player is out by failing to hit the ball on the first bounce or breaking some of the other rules (see below).

Rules

The player is out if she:

• hits the ball with anything other than with both hands, fingers pointing downwards

• hits the ball onto a line

• allows the ball to bounce more than once in their own square

• does not reach another player's quadrant

• hits the ball to a player standing outside the square

• hits the ball outside the marked area

Copyright material from Thérèse Hoyle (2021), 101 Playground Games: A Collection of Active and Engaging Playtime Games for Children, Routledge.

153

The player who is out goes to the waiting line and a new player comes into square one, while the other players move on one place. The aim is to stay in the game for as long as possible.

Variations

Use six or nine squares; this caters for more players.

Comments

This is also known as Square Ball.

92. Caught You (China)

Time: 10 minutes
Age Range: 7–11
Ideal Number of Players: 20–30
Equipment Needed: A blindfold and a small ball

How to Play

All the players sit in a circle except for one who is 'on' and sits just a few feet away from the circle with her eyes blindfolded.

Everybody passes the ball around.

When the blindfolded player shouts 'Stop!' the player who has the ball in her hand has to stand up and sing a song or tell a story.

The blindfolded player has to guess who it is. They have three guesses to get it right. If they guess correctly, they swap places with the player who sang the song and the game starts again. If they guess incorrectly, they are the blindfolded player again.

Variations

When the blindfolded player shouts 'Stop!' the player who has the ball in her hand has to stand up and disguise her voice. The blindfolded player has to guess who it is. She remains blindfolded until she has guessed correctly.

93. Clap Ball (Cameroon)

Time: 10 minutes
Age Range: 8–11
Ideal Number of Players: 12
Equipment Needed: A ball

How to Play

This is a rhythmic clapping game.

Two teams are selected, and they line up parallel and facing each other four metres from either side of a centreline.

One player starts by throwing a ball (or grapefruit or orange) to someone on the other side. All the players clap as he throws and when the ball is caught they stamp their feet.

This is then repeated, and anyone who drops a catch returns it to the thrower, who throws it again.

It is said that nobody wins or loses in this game; it is played for the joy and rhythm.

Variations

There is a competitive version of this game. When the ball is caught, the catcher must clap his hands and stamp his feet once. If a player forgets to clap and stamp, a point is scored against his team. Keep the ball moving fast.

This game can be played with a smaller space with younger players.

94. Korebe (Turkey)

Time: 8 minutes
Age Range: 4–8
Ideal Number of Players: 5–10
Equipment Needed: Blindfold

How to Play

At the start of the game one person is chosen to be 'it' and they are blindfolded.

When the game starts, the person who is 'it' tries to catch the other players.

If someone is caught, that child becomes the new 'it' and the game starts over again.

Comments

This works best in a very restricted area.

95. Ambulance (Sweden)

Time: 15 minutes
Age Range: 10
Ideal Number of Players: 10–20
Equipment Needed: None

How to Play

Mark out the boundaries for the game – a tennis or netball court is a good size.

Designate the position of the 'hospital'.

One player is 'it'. One player is the doctor. The rest of the players attempt to avoid being caught in the play area by the player who is 'it'.

When a player is caught, they become a 'victim'. The victim must lie on the ground, waiting for the 'ambulance'.

The objective is then to transport the victim to the hospital as soon as possible. Four players gather around the victim and take him to hospital. These four, as a group, become the ambulance and each individual is a wheel and they move the victim to the hospital.

None of the ambulance players can be caught if they are holding the victim.

When the ambulance and victim arrive at the hospital, they are released by the doctor to rejoin the game.

The game ends when all the players become victims or are just too tired to carry on playing.

Comments

This game is a little like 'hospital tag'.

96. Catch the Chicks (Taiwan)

Time: 10 minutes
Age Range: 5–11
Ideal Number of Players: 20
Equipment Needed: None

How to Play

The players agree on the area of the playground to be used. A netball court or a box-shaped space works well. Alternatively, mark a box out with chalk or cones.

To play the game, someone is chosen to be an eagle and someone to be a hen. The rest of the players are chicks.

The game starts with the chicks staying behind mother hen who tries to protect them while the eagle tries to catch one.

The eagle can move anywhere around the chosen space, but the mother hen will always try to block the path of the eagle so that the eagle cannot steal her chicks. The eagle must always go around mother hen when trying to steal her chicks.

To make this game more fun, the chicks can choose to move away from mother hen and then they can run around freely and tease the eagle.

If a chick sees that the eagle is about to catch him, he can crouch down and put his hands over his ears – this is a sign of an apology to the eagle and he then can't steal the chick. However, as soon as the chick gets up, the eagle can try again.

The game continues until a chick is caught. They then become the eagle, and the game starts again.

Variations

This game is also called Eagle and Chicks.

97. Sardines (Germany)

Time: 15–30 minutes
Age Range: 5–11
Ideal Number of Players: 5+
Equipment Needed: Chalk

How to Play

Mark out a home base with chalk or choose any clearly marked spot, such as a tree or bench.

Select one player to be 'it'.

The rest of the team count to 50 while 'it' goes and hides.

When the players have finished counting, they split up and go in search of 'it'.

When someone comes across 'it', she joins him in his space by squeezing into the hiding space, like a sardine, next to him.

As the remaining searchers discover the hiders, each squeezes into the hiding space. Everyone then has to be very quiet, so as not to alert the remaining searchers, which is easier said than done!

The hiding players wait for the last searching player, who is usually getting pretty nervous by this time. When he finally discovers the hiding sardines, they all jump out and race for home base. The last player to reach home base becomes the next 'it' in the next game.

98. Daaba Doobi (Pakistan)

Time: 10–15 minutes
Age Range: 6–9
Ideal Number of Players: 10+
Equipment Needed: A soft ball, bean bag or cushion

How to Play

This game can be played with a soft ball, a bean bag or a cushion.

One player throws the ball or alternative object to another player with the aim of trying to touch him with the ball.

That player must try to dodge the ball and try and catch it instead.

If they catch the ball, then they throw the ball to try to hit another player and so on.

When the ball touches another player, he is out. If, however, he catches the ball after it has touched him, he continues to play.

Comments

If playing with a ball, make sure it is a very soft ball.

99. Countries (Romania)

Time: 15 minutes
Age Range: 7–11
Ideal Number of Players: 12–30
Equipment Needed: A ball

How to Play

The players sit in a circle.

A leader is chosen. She gives each player in the circle the name of a country, for example, Spain, England, France, Germany, Turkey, Italy and so on, repeating these countries until all players are named.

She then sits in the middle of the circle with a ball in her hand.

She then throws the ball in the air, calling the name of a country.

The aim is for one child from that country to catch the ball before it bounces.

The winner is the person who catches the ball the most often.

Variations

At the start of the game, the players can participate in a round with each person selecting a different country from a specified selection of countries.

Comments

It is best to have a maximum of three people having the same country.

100. Dakpanay (Philippines)

Time: 10 minutes
Age Range: 6–10
Ideal Number of Players: 2–6
Equipment Needed: Chalk

How to Play

Players draw five circles, three metres in diameter on the ground.

The players have to run around the circles while a chaser tries to catch them.

The circles are a home/safe zone and players cannot be tagged by the chaser if they go inside these circles.

Players can only be tagged when running outside the circles.

Whoever is caught becomes the next chaser.

Comments

Limit the amount of time the players can stay in the home/safe zone.

101. Match My Feet (Democratic Republic of Congo)

Time: 10+ minutes
Age Range: 7–11
Ideal Number of Players: 10
Equipment Needed: None

How to Play

The players make a circle and one player is chosen to be the leader.

One player stands in the middle.

The leader starts off by clapping a special rhythm that they have chosen and everyone copies.

Then the player in the middle stands in front of the leader and performs a dance. When he finishes, the leader tries to imitate the dance.

Then the leader goes into the middle, the person in the middle moves back into the circle and another leader is chosen.

The new leader starts up a new clapping rhythm and everyone copies and the game continues.

Training Available from Thérèse Hoyle Consultancies

Would you like to reinvigorate your playtimes and make playtimes fun for everyone?

At Thérèse Hoyle Consultancies we support primary schools to dramatically improve the quality of day-to-day playtimes and lunchtimes, with a consequent beneficial impact on lunchtime behaviour, engagement, learning and social, emotional, mental and physical health and wellbeing. In fact, some schools have seen their serious behavioural problems completely disappear!

The following training is available as INSET, Working in School Days or online training programmes:

- **Positive Playtime Programme**. A whole-school approach to creating positive and harmonious playtimes. This is our most popular training option. We come into your school over two to three days and work with your children and whole school team. https ://theresehoyle.com/positive-playtimes/.

- **How to Be a Lunchtime Supervisor Superhero.** This is a half- or one-day workshop for lunchtime supervisors which can take place during a normal school day, as online training or as an INSET training day or twilight. https://theresehoyle.com/product /lunchtime-supervisors-superhero-training/.

- **Traditional Playground Games Workshop.** Traditional playground games have historically been handed down from generation to generation. Sadly, they are disappearing fast. Our cross-curricular workshop is aimed at teaching children games and re-inspiring your staff.

- **Positive Playtime Online Training Academy.** Join our online academy and get weekly inspiration and access to all our online training videos, resources and much, much more. Go to www.theresehoyle.com to find out more.

- **Staff Wellbeing.** A wellbeing at work programme for balancing work and life and creating a whole-school culture and shared vision of staff wellbeing.

Appendix

- **Flourishing Schools Training.** A whole-school wellbeing programme which supports positive mental health and builds social, emotional and behavioural skills with children and adults. A great day without having to close the school. We come into your school during an ordinary school day and work with staff in the classroom and playground.

Training is available worldwide.

Email: therese@theresehoyle.com

Tel: 08003 118991 or 02136 91998

Website: www.theresehoyle.com

Books and Resources Available from Thérèse Hoyle Consultancies

101 Wet Playtime Games by Thérèse Hoyle

This is the follow-up book to *101 Playground Games* and an invaluable resource to support your staff and children during wet playtimes. This book is jam-packed with activities, games, photocopiable resources and a wealth of easy-to-implement ideas. *101 Wet Playtime Games* includes easy-to-run games, a wealth of creative ideas, a selection of photocopiable resources to fill the wet play box and ideas to help implement a wet play policy.

How to Be a Peaceful School, edited by Anna Lubelska

Peace is needed now more than ever in schools, by pupils and teachers alike. This inspiring guide provides primary, secondary and special schools with practical methods to improve pupil and teacher wellbeing, combat bullying and promote peace both inside and outside the school gates. Thérèse Hoyle is a contributing author of this book and her exciting chapter, 'Peaceful Playtimes', is jam-packed with ideas and advice to transform your lunchtimes and playtimes.

Free Playground Games Toolkits

Free Traditional Playground Games Starter Kit, taken from *101 Playground Games*. Download the free Playground Games Starter Kit and you will get ten traditional games that don't require any equipment so you can start playing them with your children today.

Download the Traditional Playground Games Starter Kit: https://theresehoyle.com/free-playground-games/.

Free Primary Playtime Games Toolkit with Wet Playtime Activities taken from *101 Wet Playtime Games and Activities* by Thérèse Hoyle.

Keep pupils entertained during playtime whatever the weather with the Primary Playtime Toolkit. Suitable for children ages 4–11. This toolkit contains ten activities that can be used with pupils in and outside the classroom.

Download the Primary Playtime Toolkit: https://theresehoyle.com/free-playground-games-2/

Thérèse Hoyle's Positive Playtime Shop

For a selection of resources such as playground activity leader (PAL) tabards, playtime audit, playtime reward pads, playtime sanction pads, certificates, restorative practice worksheets, a guide to constructing a playtime behaviour policy, books and resources to support the implementation of all Thérèse Hoyle's programmes, visit https://theresehoyle.com /shop/.

Other Useful Websites

Skipping Resources

Jump Rope for Heart Fundraising Pack

Jump Rope for Heart is the British Heart Foundation's exciting skipping event that can be held at any time of year at your school or youth group.

Sign up for free, receive £100 worth of skipping equipment to help your children get more active and fundraise for the British Heart Foundation's lifesaving heart research.

www.bhf.org.uk/how-you-can-help/fundraise/schools-and-young-people-fundraising/jump -rope

British Rope Skipping Association

www.brsa.org.uk

Singing and Dancing Games – Nursery Rhyme, Lyrics, Origins and History

This website has a collection of nursery rhymes and describes their origins and the historical significance of many of the rhymes.

www.rhymes.org.uk/

Appendix

Playground Resources and Equipment

Edventure

Edventure is a major supplier of playtime equipment to two-thirds of all UK primary schools.

They specialise in the design, manufacture and supply of playtime games and equipment to schools throughout the UK.

Tel: 01323 501040

Email: sales@edventure.co.uk

Website: www.edventure.co.uk

Pentagon Play

The number one school playground specialist, Pentagon Play is an award-winning designer of outdoor learning environments and trusted by schools and nurseries across the country.

Tel (North): 01625 890330

Tel (South): 01173 790899

Email: info@pentagonplay.co.uk

Website: www.pentagonplay.co.uk/

Playdale Playgrounds

Play solutions for all ages. This company manufactures a range of playground systems and equipment.

Tel: 01539531561

Email: info@playdale.co.uk

Website: www.playdale.co.uk

Useful Organisations

Play England

Play England's aim is for all children and young people in England to have regular access and opportunity for free, inclusive, local play provision and play space.

Play England provides advice and support to promote good practice and works to ensure that the importance of play is recognised by policymakers, planners and the public.

Email: info@playengland.net

Website: www.playengland.org.uk

V&A Museum of Childhood

The V&A Museum of Childhood is the UK's first national museum designed by, and for, young people – a place where they can learn, create and debate together, and design for tomorrow.

Tel: 020 8983 5200

Fax: 020 8983 5225

Email: moc@vam.ac.uk

Website: www.vam.ac.uk/moc/index.html

Learning through Landscapes

Learning through Landscapes helps schools and early-years settings make the most of their outdoor spaces for play and learning.

Tel: 01962 846258

Website: www.ltl.org.uk

Books with More Ideas for Games, Play and Creativity

Good Practice in Playwork by P. Bonel & J. Lindon. Cheltenham: Stanely Thornes Ltd.

Great Games to Play with Groups: A Leader's Guide by F. Harris. Illinois: Fearon Teacher Aids.

Appendix

Games, Games, Games by R. Dewar, K. Palser, M. Notley & A. Piercy. London: Woodcraft Folk.

Let's Co-operate by M. Masheder. London: Green Print.

Let's Play Together, 300 Co-operative Games by M. Masheder. London: Green Print.

Parachute Games by L. Barbarash. Leeds: Human Kinetics.

Parachute Games with DVD by T. Strong and D. N. Le Fevre. Leeds: Human Kinetics.

Positively Mother Goose by D. Loomans, K. Kolberg & J. Loomans. Novato CA: HJ Kramer Inc, c/o New World Library.

The Spirit of Play by D. N. Le Fevre. Scotland: Findhorn Press.

Play by Stuart Brown. New York: Penguin.

Cooperative Games by Dada Maheshvarananda. Puerto Rico: Inner World.

Armstrong, N. & Welsman, J. R. (1997) *Young People and Physical Activity.* Oxford: Oxford University Press.

Asthana, A. & Revill, J. (2008) *Is it Time to Let Children Play Outdoors Once More?* London: Observer Newspaper.

Baines, E. & Blatchford, P. (2019) *School Break and Lunch Times and Young People's Social Lives: A Follow-Up National Study.* London: Nuffield Foundation. UCL. Institute of Education.

Basch Charles (2011) Healthier Students Make Better Learners. https://healthyschoolscampaign.org/wp-content/uploads/2017/03/A-Missing-Link-in-School-Reforms-to-Close-the-Achievement-Gap.pdf

Bouchard, C., Malina, R. M. & Perusse, L. (1997) *Genetics of Fitness and Physical Performance.* Illiniois: Human Kinetics.

British Medical Association (2005) *Preventing Childhood Obesity.* London: British Medical Association.

Broadhead, P. (2004) *Early Years Play and Learning: Developing Social Skills and Cooperation.* London: Routledge.

Brown, S. (2010) *Play.* New York: Penguin.

Burdette, H. L. & Whitaker, R. C. (2005) Resurrecting Free Play in Young Children Looking Beyond Fitness and Fatness to Attention, Affiliation, and Affect. *Archives of Paediatrics & Adolescent Medicine*, 159(1): 46–50.

Burghardt, G. M. (2005) *The Genesis of Animal Play: Testing the Limits.* Cambridge, MA: MIT Press.

Davey, G. B. (2006) Umbrella Feet: Children's Folklore and The National Library. *National Library of Australia News.* September 2006, XVI(12).

DCSF (2007) *The Children's Plan: Building Brighter Futures.* London: The Stationery Office.

Department of Health and Social Care (2019) *UK Chief Medical Officers' Physical Activity Guidelines.* London: Crown Copyright.

DFES (2004) *Every Child Matters: Change for Children in School.*

DFES (2005) *Excellence and Enjoyment: Social and Emotional Aspects of Learning.*

Dishman, R. K. (1986) *Physical Activity & Wellbeing.* Seefeldt, V. (ed.) Reston, VA: National Association for Sport and Physical Education. ED 289 874.

Doyle, W. (2017) What Australia Can Learn from Finland's Forested Classrooms. *Sydney Morning Herald*, 17 January 2017. www.smh.com.au/opinion/secrets-of-the-worlds-best-schools-fifteen-minutes-of-play-every-hour-20170116-gtrztp.html.

Follett, M. (2017) *Creating Excellence in Primary School Playtimes.* London: Jessica Kingsley.

Fluegelman, A. & Tembeck, S. (eds) (1976) *New Games Book.* New York: Bantam Doubleday Dell Publishing Group. This book is currently out of print.

Frost, J., Wortham, S. & Reifel, S. (2005) *Play and Child Development.* Upper Saddle River, NJ: Merrill Prentice-Hall.

Garner, A., Hirsh-Pasek, K., Hutchinson, J. & Golinkoff, R. M. (2018) *The Power of Play: A Pediatric Role in Enhancing Development in Young Children.* American Academy of Pediatrics. https://pediatrics.aappublications.org/content/142/3/e20182058/tab-article-info.

Gill, T. (2007) *No Fear: Growing Up in a Risk-Averse Society.* London: Calouste Gulbenkian Foundation. www.rethinkingchildhood.com.

Gill, T. (2014) *The Play Return.* Scotland: Children's Play Policy Forum.

Gopnik, A., Meltzoff, A. N. & Kuhl, P. K. (1999) *The Scientist in the Crib: What Early Learning Tells Us about the Mind.* New York: HarperCollins.

Gruber, J. J. (1986) *Physical Activity and Self-Esteem Development in Children: A Metaanalysis.* United States: American Academy of Physical Education Papers.

Health Education Authority (HEA) (1997) *Young People and Physical Activity: A Literature Review.* London: Health Education Authority.

Holden, R. (1999) *Laughter, the Best Medicine.* London: Thorsons.

Hood, L. & Malinauskas, R. (2008) *Schools Cut Lunch Break to Curb Bullies.* Melbourne, Australia: Herald Sun.

Bibliography

Hoyle, T. (2018) *How to Be a Peaceful School*. London: Jessica Kingsley Publishers.

Johnson, J. E., Christie, J. F. & Wardle, F. (2005) *Play, Development and Early Education*. Boston, MA: Pearson Education.

Le Fevre, D. N. (2006) *Parachute Games*. Leeds: Human Kinetics.

Le Fevre, D. N. (2007) *The Spirit of Play*. Scotland: Findhorn Press.

Lester, S. & Russell, W. (2007 & 2008) *Play for a Change*. London: Play England. National Children's Bureau.

Lindsey, P. & Palmer, D. (1981) *Games Children Play*. Canberra, ACT: Department for Education.

Loomans, D., Kolberg, K. & Loomans, J. (1991) *Positively Mother Goose*. Novato, CA: HJ Kramer Inc., c/o New World Library.

Lubelska, A. (2018) *How to Be a Peaceful School*. London: Jessica Kingsley Publishers.

Maheshvarananda, D. (2017) *Cooperative Games for a Cooperative World: Facilitating Trust, Communication and Spiritual Connection*. Puerto Rico: InnerWorld Publications.

Mail Online (2013) Parents' Anxieties Keep Children Playing Indoors: Fears about Traffic and Strangers Leading to 'Creeping Disappearance' of Youngsters from Parks. www.dailymail.co.uk/news/article-23 85722/Parents-anxieties-children-playing-indoors-Fears-traffic-strangers-leading-creeping-disappearance-y oungsters-parks.html.

Masheder, M. (1997) *Let's Play Together*. Guilford: Green Print.

Mental Health Foundation (2021) London. www.mentalhealth.org.uk/a-to-z/c/children-and-young-people.

Murray, R. & Ramstetter, C. (2013) The Crucial Role of Recess in School. The American Academy of Pediatrics. *AAP News and Journals. Paediatrics, Council of School Health*, 131(1): 183–188; DOI: https://doi.org/10.1542/peds.2012-2993, https://pediatrics.aappublications.org/content/131/1/183.

National Health Service (2020) *Statistics on Obesity, Physical Activity and Diet*. England.

National Union of Teachers (2007) *Time to Play*. London: National Union of Teachers.

Opie, I. (1996) Playground Rhymes and the Oral Tradition. In *International Companion Encyclopedia of Children's Literature*. Edited by Peter Hunt. London: Routledge.

Opie, I. & Opie, P. (1969) *Games in Street and Playground*. London: Oxford University Press.

Panksepp, J. (1993) Rough and Tumble Play: A Fundamental Brain Process. In *Parents and Children Playing*. Edited by MacDonald. Albany, NY: Suny Press, 147–184.

Panksepp, J. & Ikemoto, S. (1992) The Effects of Early Isolation on Motivation for Social Play in Juvenile Rats. *Developmental Psychbiology*, 24(4): 261–274.

Parish, A.M. (2013) The Effect of School Recess Interventions on Physical Activity: A Systematic Review. www.researchgate.net/publication/236064349_The_Effect_of_School_Recess_Interventions_on_Physical_Act ivity_A_Systematic_Review.

Patte, M. (2006, October) What's Happened to Recess: Examining Time Devoted to Recess in Pennsylvania's Elementary Schools. *Play & Folklore*, 48(6).

Pellegrini, A. (2005) *Recess: Its Role in Education and Development*. New Jersey: Lawrence Erlbaum Associates, Inc.

Pellegrini, A., et al. (1995) A Developmental Contextualist Critique of Attention Deficit/Hyperactivity Disorder. *Educational Researcher*, 24(1): 13–20.

Pellegrini, A. et al. (1996) The effects of children's playground and classroom behaviours. *American Educational Research Journal*, 32(4): 845–864.

Play England (2013) www.dailymail.co.uk/news/article-2385722/Parents-anxieties-children-playing-indoors-F ears-traffic-strangers-leading-creeping-disappearance-youngsters-parks.html.

Play England (2021) Why Play is Important. Bristol. www.playengland.org.uk/about-us/why-play-is-import ant/.

Playday (2007) *Our Streets Too!* London: National Children's Bureau. www.playday.org.uk/resources/resear ch/2007-research/.

Ridgers, N.D. et al. (2007) Children's Physical Activity Levels during School Recess: A Quasi-Experimental Intervention Study. *International Journal of Behavioral Nutrition and Physical Activity*, 4: 19.

Schachter, R. (2005) The End of Recess. *District Administration*, 41(8): 36.

Sharp, S. & Smith, P. (1991–1993) *Tackling Bullying: The Sheffield Project in Understanding and Managing Bullying*. Oxford: Heinemann Educational.

Siraj-Blatchford, I. & Sylva, K. (2004) Researching Pedagogy in English Pre-schools. *British Education Journal*, 30(5): 713–730.

Smith, P. K. & Sharp, S. (eds) (1994) *School Bullying: Insights and Perspectives*. London: Routledge.

Sunderland, M. (2016) *The Science of Parenting*. London: Dorling Kindersley.

Sutton-Smith, B. (2003) Play as a Parody of Emotional Vulnerability. In *Play and Educational Theory and Practise, Play and Culture Studies*, Vol. 5. Edited by J. L. Roopnarine. Westport, CT.

The Best Schools (2019) *The Death of Recess in America.* https://thebestschools.org/magazine/death-of-recess/.

The Children's Society (2007) *Reflection on Childhood; Part of the Good Childhood Inquiry – What You Told Us about Friends.* www.childrenssociety.org.uk.

The Guardian (2016) Three-Quarters of UK Children Spend Less Time Outdoors Than Prison Inmates. www.theguardian.com/environment/2016/mar/25/three-quarters-of-uk-children-spend-less-time-outdoors-than-prison-inmates-survey

The Parliamentary Office of Science and Technology (2003) *Improving Children's Diet.* Report 199. London: POST.

The Sydney Morning Herald (2016) *This is Why Finland Has the Best Schools.* www.smh.com.au/national/this-is-why-finland-has-the-best-schools-20160325-gnqv9l.html.

Times Education Supplement (1997) *Give Them Enough Ropes.* London: Times Education.

UNICEF (2013) *Report Card 11: An Overview of Child Wellbeing in Rich Countries.* www.unicef-irc.org/publications/pdf/rc11_eng.pdf.

Verstraete, S. (2006) *Increasing Children's Physical Activity Levels during Recess Periods in Elementary Schools: The Effects of Providing Game Equipment.* National Library of Medicine. https://pubmed.ncbi.nlm.nih.gov/16431866/

Wenner, M. (2009) The Serious Need to Play. *The Scientific American Mind*, 28 January 2009.

United Nations Convention on the Rights of the Child (1989). www.ohchr.org.

Waring, M. et al. (2007) Observation of Children's Physical Activity Levels in Primary School: Is the School an Ideal Setting for Meeting Government Activity Targets? https://doi.org/10.1177/1356336X07072672

Wood, E. (2007) New Directions in Play: Consensus or Collision? *Education* 35(4): 309–320.

Wood, E. & Atfield, J. (2005) *Play, Learning and the Early Childhood Curriculum* (2nd Edition). London: Paul Chapman.

World Health Organisation (2021) *Physical Activity.* Geneva, Switzerland. www.who.int/news-room/fact-sheets/detail/physical-activity.

Games Template
Reward Slips
Certificate for Playing Kindly
Playground Star Award
Application Form to be a Playground Activity Leader
PAL Selection Interview Form
Playground PAL Award

Games Template

Name of Game:

Time: … Minutes
Age Range:
Ideal Number of Players:
Equipment Needed:

How to Play:

Variations:

Comments:

Reward Slips

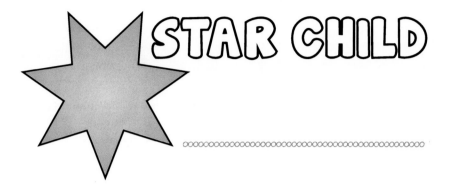

STAR CHILD

STAR PLAYER

CAUGHT BEING GOOD

CERTIFICATE FOR PLAYING KINDLY

Awarded to:

_____

THANK YOU!

Date

_____

Signed

_____

PLAYGROUND STAR AWARD

Awarded to:

_____

Date

_____

Signed

_____

APPLICATION FORM TO BE A PLAYGROUND ACTIVITY LEADER

Name: **Class:**

Why would you like to be a playground activity leader?

What qualities do you have that would make a good playground activity leader?

How do you think that becoming a playground activity leader will help you?

What games could you teach children to play?

PAL Selection Interview Form
(interviewer's questions and note sheet)

Name:	Class:

Why would you like to be a PAL?

What do you think would make you a good PAL?

What games do you know?

What do you think your role/job will involve?

Teaching traditional playground games
Helping lonely children make friends
Putting equipment out
Act as positive role models and teach the values of caring and friendship

What challenges do you think may come up? How would you deal with them?

Questions?

Need to send a letter congratulating them and outlining the job!

PLAYGROUND PAL AWARD

For outstanding help at playtimes

Awarded to:

_____

Date

_____

Signed

_____

Index

Note: Bold refers to the beginning of each section.

Index